"*Defrocked* is either the saddest book a.... the church I've read or the most hopeful. It's certainly real. Schaefer brings a pastor's heart and a pastor's wounds to his history-making memoir. There are times when I think that if we could just kick all the human beings out of the church, we could really do this Christianity thing. But of course that's the whole point. *Defrocked* reminds me why real Christian community matters, why it is hard to sustain and why it is still heroic to strive for."
— Lillian Daniel, Author of When *"Spiritual But Not Religious" Is Not Enough*, Senior Minister, First Congregational Church, Glen Ellyn, Illinois

"If the heart of the gospel is unconditional love, then why do we punish those who actually practice it? Our faith was born of resistance to loveless legalism, and Frank Schaefer's loving act of resistance is the essence of faith itself. Would that more fathers loved their sons this much. It might just save the church."
— Robin Meyers, Senior Minister, Mayflower Congregational United Church of Christ, Oklahoma City, Author of *The Underground Church: Reclaiming the Subversive Way of Jesus*

"What Frank Schaefer and his family suffered at the hands of their denomination is tragic. Be warned. *Defrocked* is a painful, close-up look at the United Methodist Church struggling to end its not-so-civil war against homosexuality and homosexuals. However, also be warned that if you don't read *Defrocked*, you will miss a rare and deeply moving opportunity to watch a truly Christian family stand united against scientific ignorance and biblical misuse and never stop loving God, their Church, their family, and even their enemies."
— Mel White, Cofounder of Soulforce and Author of *Stranger at the Gate*

"Schaefer's conviction to compassionately balance his conscience with family, LGBT social justice, and religious practice was admirable. Where many talk about the need for change inside our religious institutions, Schaefer took personal responsibility to live out his principles at great cost. Though defrocked, Schaefer's action honors the Gospel one hopes Christ's inspiration encourages us all to follow. That we would turn toward our neighbor in love rather than against and let love be the law that binds us all."

   — Jennifer Knapp, Singer/Songwriter

"As more and more people in mainstream America support the rights of gay, lesbian, bisexual, and transgendered people, it's easy to forget the heroes who stood up, spoke out, and paid a price to bring us to this point. Rev. Frank Schaefer and his family faced an unjust choice: affirm their son's commitment to the man he loved or affirm their commitment to the United Methodist Church they loved. Frank's unquestionable commitment to his faith and his courage to stand against unjust policies make him a prophetic leader of our age. Read about his remarkable journey—and find your own prophetic voice along the way."

   — Cameron Trimble, Executive Director and CEO, The Center for Progressive Renewal

"In Rev. Frank Schaefer's book *Defrocked* we meet a humble minister who, in calmer times, would have quietly lived out his faith in small town Lebanon, Pennsylvania, attending to the needs of his flock. These, however, are not those times. Faced with a gay son who asked him to preside at his wedding, Frank took a road that is still, in the Christian church of 2014, less traveled. Whether it is apparent or not, every church in America today that continues to view LGBT as equal but also separate is filled with division and inner tension: Rev. Schaefer's book gives an inside view to this conflict and how it will continue to play out for many years to come. Rev. Schaefer shows the way forward in this story with his simple, steady commitment to follow 'in His steps' to the best of his ability, each and every day."

— Randy Roberts Potts, Freelance Writer, Photographer, and out gay grandson of Oral Roberts

"Confronting our traditional beliefs about faith as it intersects sexual orientation and gender identity is a difficult process. While many of us in conservative churches are aware of the injustices suffered by LGBT believers, it seems too big a task to take on those traditions. So we comply in our actions and with our mouths, while our hearts and spirits yearn to seek truth. Until we are pushed, most of us remain complacent. More and more often, the push is coming from the gay and transgender children of conservative believers. This challenge is happening in every denomination and every state. Imagine if you are the pastor and your gay child comes to you, and, beyond loving and accepting them, requests that you perform their wedding. You are then pushed to the edges, to speak out from your silent place against the injustice. Pastor Frank Schaefer found himself in that place."

— Kathy Baldock, Author of *Walking the Bridgeless Canyon*

Frank and Brigitte Schaefer with their children—Tim, Kevin, Deborah, and Pascal—in 1999.

DEFROCKED

How a Father's
Act of Love Shook
the United Methodist Church

Franklyn Schaefer
with Sherri Wood Emmons

CHALICE
PRESS
ST. LOUIS, MISSOURI

www.ChalicePress.com

Print: 9780827244993
EPUB: 9780827244986   EPDF: 9780827244979

Library of Congress Cataloging in Publication Data available
upon request.

CONTENTS

The United Methodist Church is a part of the church universal, which is one Body in Christ. The United Methodist Church acknowledges that all persons are of sacred worth. All persons, without regard to race, color, national origin, status, or economic condition, shall be eligible to attend its worship services, participate in its programs, receive the sacraments, upon baptism be admitted as baptized members, and upon taking vows declaring the Christian faith become professing members in any local church in the connection. In The United Methodist Church no conference or other organizational unit of the Church shall be structured so as to exclude any member or any constituent body of the Church because of race, color, national origin, status or economic condition... All people may attend its worship services, participate in its programs, receive the sacraments and become members in any local church in the connection.

—Book of Discipline of the United Methodist Church,
Article IV, "Inclusiveness of the Church"

The practice of homosexuality is incompatible with Christian teaching. Therefore self-avowed practicing homosexuals are not to be certified as candidates, ordained as ministers, or appointed to serve in The United Methodist Church... Ceremonies that celebrate homosexual unions shall not be conducted by our ministers and shall not be conducted in our churches.

—Book of Discipline of the United Methodist Church,
paragraphs 304.3, 341.6.

PROLOGUE

ON NOVEMBER 19, 2013, I sat in the witness stand of a make-shift courtroom at a church camp in Eastern Pennsylvania, the same camp my children had attended years earlier. The day before, a jury of my fellow pastors had found me guilty of performing a same-sex marriage and of violating the order and discipline of The United Methodist Church.

Before the court meted out my punishment, I now had the opportunity to plead my case. I faced the very real possibility of being defrocked and losing my livelihood. My counsel had crafted a carefully worded statement for me to read before the judge and jury. But as I looked out at my family and supporters in that room, at the sea of rainbow-colored stoles gathered there, I knew I could not read it.

Instead, I spoke from my heart. I told the court I could not uphold the teachings in The United Methodist Church's *Book of Discipline* that said homosexuality was incompatible with Christian teaching. I was now and would continue to be an advocate for my gay brothers and sisters in the church and beyond. I said that I would continue to minister to *all* people equally, regardless of their gender, nationality, race, social status, economic status, or sexual orientation. And I called on the church to stop treating gay people as second-class Christians.

I did not ask to be put in an advocacy position, but there I was. My road to that place was a long one, beginning with evangelical, conservative roots. It was not a planned journey, but it became my journey—a journey redirected by an act of love for my gay son, the story of a father's love for his son.

This is my story.

DEEP ROOTS

I WAS BORN AND RAISED in Wuppertal, a mid-sized city in western Germany with a rich history, not too far from Cologne. In the years leading up to the Second World War, there was a movement within the church in Germany that was opposed to what Hitler and the Nazis were doing in the country. It's called the Confessing Church. Great theologians such as Dietrich Bonhoeffer and Karl Barth founded the Confessing Church in Germany; the Barmen Declaration, which was mostly formulated by Karl Barth, was adopted at a council meeting right there in my hometown of Barmen in the Gemarker Kirche. So we had a keen awareness of the Confessing Movement in Wuppertal. In fact, Wuppertal is the city with the most Christian denominations represented in all of Germany. And that's where I was born and raised.

Born in 1961, I grew up as a child of the Baby Boomer generation. Our classes at school were so full then. I remember in first grade, there were thirty-six children in a classroom with one teacher and no assistant. Kids were kind of invisible then. It was a time when, wherever you went as a child, you were to be seen and not heard. Even in church. Maybe especially in church.

I was not raised a Methodist. The Methodist Church is fairly small in Germany. I was baptized in the Reformed Church, where my grandparents belonged. But when I was six or seven years old, my parents joined a Baptist church after they experienced a spiritual

1

awakening, and they became very committed evangelical believers. They started to attend a Baptist church, and that's the church where I grew up and got most of my Christian education.

My mother's father, Opa August, was a part of the Confessing Church. He was furious with what was going on in Germany in the prewar years. He was totally opposed to Hitler. He wouldn't allow my mom or her sister to join the Hitler Youth, which was similar to the Girl Scouts in the United States today, but it was part of the Nazi program to "educate" the young generation. My grandfather refused to fly the flag with the swastika on it. Because of that, I was told that my grandparents' house was the only one on the block that never had any mounting for a flag. He was arrested when the Nazis found out he was opposed to the government and they threw him in jail. And it was only because he had such great standing in the community that he was released. He was an elder in the church and very well-respected.

My dad's father, Herman Schaefer, was part of the Nazi Party. I don't know how much he was involved, whether he was active or if he only belonged because he was a businessman and joined so as not to lose out on business deals. He was drafted and fought in World War II and he never came back. As far as I know, he is still officially missing in action. He was actually a Red Cross truck driver. So I want to say that, maybe, because of that, he was a Nazi in name only. Maybe that was his way of saying, "Well, if I have to be part of this war, I can do something humanitarian." I don't know this for sure, but I want to give him the benefit of the doubt.

My Opa Herman was the one who never came back from the war, so I never got to know him. My dad was only three or four years old when he saw his dad for the last time.

Even in the 1960s, Germany was a sort of post-war culture. The economic recovery happened in the 1950s, so many people were doing a lot better financially, but it was still a struggle for most families, including mine. The Nazi regime and the war had definitely left their mark. I heard gruesome war stories growing up. Every time a siren went off somewhere, it seemed the stories came out. Sirens were how they had known the bombers were coming and they had to hurry to either the community bomb shelters or their basements. There were stories about streets burning as phosphor bombs hit, charred corpses my grandparents had to step over, people lost in the rubble of their homes, children screaming.

My grandmother on my father's side, Margarete Schaefer, had to flee from the family estate in East Prussia as the war drew to a close, as Russian soldiers were rushing in. Out of fear of retaliatory acts, she fled to western Germany with four young children, along with thousands of her compatriots. She had to walk for miles pulling a cart with a few belongings and with her two younger children.

We grew up knowing their fear and how traumatic it had been for them. In Wuppertal, I believe something like 40 percent of the buildings were destroyed in RAF bombings, and the memories of the destruction were ingrained in peoples' memories. Moreover, when I was a teenager, I learned about the horrible history of the Third Reich—the systematic and brutal persecution of political enemies, homosexuals, the disabled, and especially the Jewish community. I saw the Dauchau concentration camp, and what I experienced there was life-changing. I was sick to my stomach as I looked at images and exhibits and heard unspeakable stories of human suffering, pain, and death. I could not wrap my mind around the fact that human beings had committed these unspeakable crimes against fellow human beings for no other reason than their having a different ethnic or religious background, and I could not believe that these people were my own. When I learned that a large part of the German church was either supportive of the Hitler regime or ignored the crimes committed, I became drawn to the history of the Confessing Church.

But the stories from my dad's side of the family also had a lasting impact. I learned how desperately poor they were and that my father was hospitalized several times for malnutrition, because there was not enough food. Often even children had to work in order for families to survive, which meant my dad missed a lot of school. He and his brothers would walk along the train tracks looking for bits of coal that had fallen off the wagons. "Sometimes," he told me, "when trains went by, some engineers and operators had compassion for the scrawny kids and dropped a few pieces of coal for them."

I heard how the community had pulled together to help one another, how allied soldiers, especially GIs, helped out struggling families, often at their own expense. My dad often shared that one of the reasons he didn't starve to death was an American aid program, and he spoke fondly of the "Quaker" meals he received at school. The U.S. economic program, commonly known in

Germany as *the Marshall Plan, was largely responsible for the success of the wiederaufbau (rebuilding),* which led to the economic miracle in the late 1950s. As a result, I grew up with a very positive image of the United States, even a sense of gratitude.

We are all shaped by the stories of our upbringing, and I believe those stories are at the root of my convictions and values today. I attribute many of my strongest convictions to these formative years, including my commitment to pacifism and a staunch belief that individual conscience takes priority over institutional loyalty.

My belief in the importance of an inclusive church was formed growing up in an evangelical Baptist church that was rather conservative. I remember a lot of good things from my Baptist years. I learned about the love, mercy, and forgiveness of God. But I also remember a certain theology of fear and judgment of the "world" that had an effect on me. One of the biggest questions I had was why I was not allowed to partake in communion. I understand the theology behind it now, but at the time I resented sitting in the pew as the plate and the cup were passed by me. It seemed like such an important moment in the life of the church, and I felt excluded from that holy moment because I had not officially professed Christianity yet. I remember thinking that I was not good enough to be a part of communion.

Because of exclusion I encountered in church as well as in the culture around me, I often felt unworthy to participate, unimportant. It seems a pretty common experience of the Baby Boomer generation. I believe these experiences helped shape my later approach to ministry, with an emphasis that nobody should be made to feel excluded.

So, when I became a minister, I would tell parents, "If you're comfortable with it, bring your children forward for communion, because they should not feel excluded and should be part of it. Communion is a joyful moment, it is a celebration of our faith, and our children are a big part of that celebration."

If parents weren't comfortable bringing their children to communion, I asked them to explain to them why they believed they should wait, and not just exclude them.

My parents still live in Wuppertal. As I child, we did live in a different part of Germany for about three years, and it took me a couple of years to get used to the dialect and the different attitudes and customs. I definitely felt like an outsider during that time. But

I always felt accepted and loved by my parents. My dad, Horst, was an engineer before he retired, and my mom, Christel, was an accountant. They provided a home that was deeply religious, caring, and supportive. One of my frequent complaints growing up was, "Do we always have to be the last people to leave church on Sunday mornings?" Many years later I learned that my own kids had the same complaint once I became a minister.

My brother, Uwe, is two years younger than me and, curiously, he also became a pastor and was ordained before I was. I love thinking back to our early childhood years when we were best buddies. Unfortunately, that changed when we became teenagers. Even though our relationship was tainted during those years, I knew that my experience of feeling excluded was nothing compared to his. He probably had ADHD as a child—a condition that was not well understood at that time. Instead of getting the help he needed, he was misunderstood and treated harshly, and he remembers our childhood home as being less happy.

Even though I did not understand what was going on with him and we had our fights, I remember feeling compassion for him in those moments when I felt he was unduly disciplined or rejected. I remember several instances when I put my arm around him to comfort him, and once when I stood up for him against our church's youth group. It bothered me when he was excluded or threatened with rejection, in part because I knew what it felt like—though to a much lesser degree than he.

After graduating from secondary school and while pursuing an apprenticeship to become an electronics technician, I met my wife. Brigitte visited my youth group at the Baptist church and started to attend the events regularly. I found myself drawn to her instantly, though I think the only reason I got *her* attention was my passion for playing the guitar, even though my left arm was in a cast at the time. Within three months, we had started to date, and we got married only two years later, on November 28, 1980.

Brigitte was a surgeon's assistant in a small practice, while I studied electrical engineering. And three years into our marriage, we had our first child, Tim. He was born six weeks premature and with serious medical problems. In fact, his pediatrician told us that Tim would probably not survive the blood poisoning he had developed in addition to his heart problem. Brigitte and I were devastated, but we somehow believed he would come through. We could only touch him through a port in the incubator with surgical gloves. Still, we rubbed his cheeks and his tiny body and talked to him and relied on our faith and the support of our family, friends, and church.

Around this time, Brigitte's brother and sister-in-law also had their first baby, Suzie, who also had severe medical complications. For much of their first five weeks, Suzie and Tim were in the same hospital room, separated by their incubators. When little Suzie passed away, it was heartbreaking, even while Tim survived and grew strong enough to be able to have open-heart surgery at six weeks. The procedure was successful, and we were so relieved to take Timmy home.

As a parent, I've often wondered if there were signs our son would one day turn out gay, but there weren't. Still, I believe God was already preparing us. Brigitte never really struggled with accepting homosexuality, in part because of her upbringing in a more progressive Christian home.

I, on the other hand, had been taught that homosexuality was a sin, and I accepted that teaching without questioning. That all began to change after I met my wife.

Brigitte's parents owned a building in downtown Wuppertal-Elberfeld that had about twenty rental units. Helmut and Irene were the first progressive Christians I got to know personally, and I remember being impressed at how nonjudgmental and accepting of others they were. They practiced what they believed and, as a result, rented their apartments to nontraditional families, including homosexual couples. This is how I met an "out" gay person for the first time. Herr Sieber was one of the renters whom I got to know a little. I remember thinking he was not at all the way I had envisioned homosexuals to be; he was nice and interesting to talk to. I could see myself being friends with him. When Herr Sieber died, from AIDS I believe, I was sad. I remember thinking he was far too young to die. During this time, I started to think about the Bible and homosexuality differently. I became critical of my church's condemnation of homosexuality. In talks with my friends from church, I remember saying that if it turned out that homosexuality was not a choice, the church was in trouble.

BECOMING A MINISTER

AFTER ABOUT FOUR YEARS struggling as a part-time student in Germany, I switched course and soon decided to move to the United States for six months to improve my English. When we arrived, I was twenty-eight years old and Brigitte and I had two children—Tim and Debbie. My parents connected us through their church with a family in Norfolk, Virginia—Walter and Charlotte Castine, who showed us the famous Southern hospitality. Their church family adopted us and gifted us with the biggest car we had ever laid eyes on. The whole family could sleep in this station wagon, I'm not kidding. We actually did sleep in it once on a trip. It was a gas guzzler, but we were grateful to have it.

We had more dinner invitations than we could accept from Brentwood Baptist Church, and they offered us their little empty parsonage to live in. After we moved in, we often found bags filled with groceries on our porch. It was too much! But their hospitality allowed us to extend our stay to about a year.

After a while, we moved into an apartment and started going to a lively church just down the road, where we seemed to fit a bit better. We made a lot of friends at the Ocean View Assemblies of God Church and, as we had done in the past, we got involved. I played the acoustic guitar on the worship team and sang in the choir. We also helped in the children's program. One day, the minister, Reverend Hodges, said he wanted to talk to me in his office. I thought

I must be in trouble. I had no idea what he wanted to talk with me about, but I went anyway.

He smiled at me and said, "Frank, I see something in you that makes me think God is calling you into the ministry. Have you ever considered that God is calling you to be a minister?"

And I had, long ago. But, honestly, the first thought that came to my mind was, "I'm not going back to school. I've been in school my whole life. I'm *not* going back."

Pastor Hodges laughed. "Well, just keep an open mind." Then he pulled out a catalog from an Assemblies of God college in Phoenixville, Pennsylvania. It was probably ten years old, crumpled and yellowed. "Why don't you fill out the application that's in this catalog, and just see what happens?"

I did. And I got accepted. But before deciding, I fasted for three days. There was something in me that agreed with Pastor Hodges. Outside of not wanting to go back to school, the idea of ministry reverberated with me. Then on the night of the third day, I had a vivid dream. I have not had many dreams like that, maybe only two or three in my life that I believe were divinely inspired. In this dream I was transported back in time and I saw myself as a seventeen-or-eighteen-year-old. I heard myself talking to my best friend at the time, saying to him, "You know what I would *really* like to do is go to Bible school. But I can't do that because I think I have to actually hear God's voice. You know, like a booming voice from heaven or something, because you have to have a calling for that."

As the dream continued, it was like God was saying to me, "Who do you think put that desire in your heart?" So there it was—my booming voice from heaven. I truly felt a call to become a pastor.

I talked about the decision with Brigitte. She had a big part in my decision to go back to school. When we share this story she always says, "Well, it's not what I signed up for, to be a pastor's wife." That's not what she envisioned when she married me. But she supported me then and she supports me now.

FINDING THE
METHODIST CHURCH

BEFORE I STARTED SCHOOL, we went back to Germany, and that's where our son Kevin was born. In the fall of 1990, we returned to the United States, where I began at Valley Forge Christian College.

As part of the curriculum, I had to get familiar with work in a church in some capacity. I earned my "ministry points" in a Methodist church, which was my first encounter with Methodism.

The Elverson United Methodist Church invited me to become their first youth minister. It was part-time, of course, much like a student intern position. I worked with both the children and the youth. They had just started growing, in large part because of the new pastor from the nearby Valley Forge Christian College. A Pentecostal professor became the pastor of a United Methodist church because Elverson Church lacked finances, and he brought in students like me from the college to help. Before long, it became a thriving church.

Tom, the pastor, became my mentor and my time there was a great experience for me and my family. I felt like I was going back to my Reformed roots, the faith tradition of my grandparents. I had never really been immersed in the traditional part of worship before, because the Baptist church I attended as a child was more informal than traditional. But, at Elverson, I found myself appreciating the ancient prayers, the Doxology, the Lord's Prayer, and the liturgical parts of the service.

But what I appreciated most at Elverson was the diversity and openness that seemed characteristic of The United Methodist Church, especially this particular church. Because they had been in a decline for so many years and had faced the threat of having to close their doors, they were open to more contemporary aspects of worship. So we had a good blended worship experience at the church. I was excited to be a part of several interesting ministries and worship styles, and there was great variety. I began to think I could see myself as a United Methodist minister. The whole Elverson experience—the growth and the interactions between the younger and the older folks—it just worked. It was magical. I remember thinking, "Wow, the Methodist Church has something going."

So, in 1993, at the end of my studies in Valley Forge and after I had been accepted into the master of divinity program at Princeton Theological Seminary, I called up the bishop of the Eastern Pennsylvania region, Bishop Susan Morrison. I was naïve and thought, *I'm just going to call the bishop and see if they want me or need me or whatever.* So, just like that, I got to talk to a bishop. I told my whole story about my eclectic background—the Reformed, the Baptist, the Pentecostal, and the Charismatic—and how I loved working at Elverson. And at the end of my spiel—I must have talked for several minutes—she simply said, "Welcome to The United Methodist Church." Just like that, I had found a church home where I could become a minister.

Bishop Morrison sent me to Morrisville United Methodist Church as student pastor in the Eastern Pennsylvania conference, where I could serve during my studies at Princeton. I commuted back and forth and we lived in the parsonage. Because Princeton is such an endowed school, I qualified for a need-based scholarship, which paid for the entire cost, so I never had to take out any major loans, and that was a total "God thing."

Now we had three children—Tim, Deborah, and Kevin—and while we were living in the Morrisville parsonage, we had our fourth child, Pascal. His birth was a *major* event in the church. The Morrisville congregation just loved that one of their student pastors had a young family and a brand new baby. Pascal was so spoiled by the church folks. He had every toy you can think of, every amenity for a baby. It was amazing.

I loved being a student pastor, because as a student pastor you can't really do anything wrong in the minds of the people. The congregation forgave every mistake I made. I often heard people make excuses for my mess ups, saying things like, "Well, one day he'll be a great minister." We often think back to the good times at Morrisville. It was such a supportive congregation. The experienced affirmed my call to ministry in the Methodist Church.

MY SON IS GAY

AFTER I RECEIVED MY master's of divinity degree in 1996, I was ordained in The United Methodist Church. Back then, it was a two-step process. You were ordained as a deacon first. As a deacon, you had all the duties and rights of a pastor, but you were still a probationary member of the annual conference.

So, I had to go through a two-year probationary time and more training, followed by a big church exam. And, finally, after passing the final interview I was ordained an elder in 1998. Eventually, the church did away with that system because it doesn't actually make sense to be ordained twice.

My first ordination was amazing, probably even more special to me than the second one because Susan Morrison, the bishop who had called me into ministry in The United Methodist Church, was part of it. She had been moved to another conference shortly before the ceremony. Peter Weaver was the new bishop who presided over the ceremony, but Susan came back for the ordination ceremony and actually washed my feet as part of the liturgical ritual, which felt very special to me. About a month later, I started my first solo appointment in a small church in Lebanon, Pennsylvania.

For five years I pastored at the Avon Zion United Methodist Church. We lived in the parsonage of the church. It was a small congregation, and when we first arrived it was struggling financially. The first three months, there wasn't enough income to support my full salary, as attendance was between thirty and forty on an average Sunday morning. So, I accepted partial pay checks until the financial situation improved.

The Avon Zion church had undergone a conflict before my time. As membership and income had declined, the leadership of the church had been in conversation with the district superintendent about possibly closing its doors. A few months before my arrival, a 24-hour community prayer vigil for the survival of the church had been held. The situation did not scare me; I was able to draw from the experience at Elverson United Methodist Church, where I had witnessed firsthand how a church can come back to life.

I began to introduce contemporary songs, which I accompanied on my acoustic guitar. I introduced drama and other contemporary worship elements, which created a blended worship style that started to attract our neighbors from the community.

Things were in such a desperate financial state in the beginning that I felt I had to resort to drastic outreach measures. I thought up some attention-getting events and communicated with the local press, which landed the church on the front page of the *Lebanon Daily News* as well as the *Harrisburg Patriot News*.

I remember preaching to the congregation from a boat (as Jesus did) on our Church Picnic Sunday at Mt. Gretna (a United Methodist camp). I preached a "comedy sermon" one Sunday, and on Palm Sunday I brought a live donkey into the sanctuary. I constructed a paper mâché whale out of pool noodles, blankets, and newsprint when I preached about Jonah one Sunday. For one baptism, I brought into the sanctuary a commercial tub so we could have a baptism by immersion, which is not something Methodists usually do.

Together with the church's newly founded worship band, I led a service for inmates at the Lebanon County prison once a month. I would be remiss not to credit the Avon congregation with much of the growth that resulted from our outreach efforts. I think once a congregation has been to the brink of closure, there is a keen sense of how important it is to welcome visitors. I was amazed at how cordially visitors were greeted and welcomed into the church. Within my two or three years at the Avon Church, attendance rose to about 120 on an average Sunday. New members were welcomed into the leadership of the church, which allowed us to revive programs such as a children's music ministry, an annual bazaar, family events, and a fall festival.

It was at the height of my ministry at the Avon Church that I learned that my oldest son, Tim, is gay.

I was in the church office when I received a phone call from a woman who said she wanted to remain anonymous. She said she was very concerned for Tim, who was seventeen years old at the time. She wanted me to know that Tim was gay and that he was struggling with his sexual orientation. In fact, she said, Tim was having suicidal thoughts.

I think there was somebody else in the church waiting to meet with me, so I couldn't talk long. I remember, though, being in denial at first. I couldn't believe that Tim was gay. But I thanked the woman for calling me. Then I went home and I talked to my wife. And Brigitte also didn't think it was probable that Tim was gay. We didn't know what to do with that phone call. But we were very concerned about it, especially about the report of the suicidal thoughts. And so we decided that we had to ask him for ourselves. We just had to ask him.

So we simply asked him. And he said, "Yes, it's true. I'm gay."

Then he told us about his struggle. And oh, he had struggled. He had cried himself to sleep many, many times, praying to God, asking God to make him "normal," to take away the homosexual desire that he felt. And when that didn't happen, he thought it might be better for him to be gone—that it might be better for his dad, the minister, and his family, and his community.

Faith was always important to Tim. From early on, he was very involved in the church. He was an active youth group member; he preached on Youth Sundays; he did special music in church and was part of the worship band. His faith was important to him. And that faith was now causing him so much pain.

When he was about twelve or thirteen years old, I had taken Tim along to our annual church conference, where we listened to a debate about homosexuality. I didn't know it then, but he was already struggling with his sexual orientation. And for him to hear people at that conference, people from his own faith tradition, say that homosexuality or the practice of homosexuality is a sin, that it is an abomination—that was devastating for him.

I remember that it was a fierce debate. Some of the things that were said were very, very hurtful. I didn't experience them as hurtful at the time because I didn't know then that my son was gay. So in a sense I was emotionally disconnected from the issue. But I remember the debate was very emotionally charged. People got very passionate—even angry—on both sides.

I remember talking to Tim about the debate at the time. From a very early age, he had been interested in politics; in fact, he ended up studying political science. I thought at the time that the annual church conference had been an interesting experience for him, a chance to see the church working democratically through a hard issue. Instead, he had learned for the first time that the church, *his* church, actually thought of him as a "freak." I'm sure it took him a while to process what all this meant when he heard those messages. But he certainly perceived them as hateful messages, hateful messages from his own church, the only faith tradition that he knew.

So Tim started to struggle from that point forward, until he came to the point where he seriously considered suicide. In fact, he shared with us later that he had actually thought about ways of doing it. So it was very serious.

As we listened to Tim tell his story that day, my wife and I were in tears. We just couldn't believe what we were hearing. We had noticed that he seemed depressed before. But we hadn't realized how severe it was. We had noticed that he'd become sort of withdrawn. When he came home from work or from school, he would go straight up to his room. But we thought, "Well, it's a phase. Kids go through that." We had no idea what he was going through.

And that was part of the pain Brigitte and I felt. All that time, all those years, he'd kept this to himself. He didn't even feel comfortable talking to us about it. Fortunately, he did confide in a friend. And the mother of that friend, we think, was the one who actually called me in the church office.

My wife and I were in tears. We hugged Tim and told him that we loved him, and that it didn't matter to us that he was gay. And then we started to affirm him. We said things like, "You were made in the image of God, gay and all. Obviously you didn't choose this. So, this is the way God created you."

Tim's story was the ultimate proof to me that homosexuality is *not* a choice. And as I fully realized this, I felt the need to counter what our general church culture conveyed in terms of homosexuality being sinful. I remember saying to him, "There is nothing wrong or sinful about being homosexual. This is who you are. God created you this way and God is proud of you. So be proud of yourself for who you are."

Still, for years to come Tim would struggle with his identity as a gay man. I remember him saying things like, "If there were a switch I could flip somewhere in my body to make me heterosexual, I'd do it."

At one point, Tim became intrigued with the Exodus program, the ministry that claimed to help people "overcome" homosexuality through prayer and therapy. I'm pretty sure he knew the program could not possibly work, but I think he wished it were possible.

In many ways, Tim is a very traditional guy. He thought about having a family with kids, he wanted the traditional "American dream." It took him many years to become comfortable with himself, the man God had created him to be.

While I embraced my son and affirmed him, I was struggling internally with his coming out. This was in 2000, and at that time being gay was even less accepted than it is today. So part of the struggle was the fear that Tim would have to face ridicule, persecution, and discrimination.

I had become very tolerant toward lesbian/gay/bisexual/transgender (LGBT) issues during my seminary time. Not that I took any human sexuality classes; I'm not even sure they were offered. It was through my own personal efforts to really search out the Bible on the passages people use to denounce homosexuality, in part because some of my fellow seminarians were openly gay and pursuing pastoral careers. During that time, I discovered that there were a number of biblical scholars who offered alternative interpretations to the literal interpretation of those passages. I learned that the authors of the various "homophobic" passages most certainly did not have a modern concept of a committed, loving relationship between same-gendered persons in mind.

This study helped me rethink the issue of homosexuality from a biblical perspective. But there's a difference between theoretically accepting it and learning that one of your own children is gay. And that was still an internal struggle for me.

I probably had all the common questions parents of gay children ask. "Did I fail in my fatherly duties? Is there something I did or didn't do that caused my son to be gay?" When you learn your child is gay, you have to readjust all your hopes and expectations. I remember mourning the fact that we were probably not going to have biological grandchildren from Tim. And I had to overcome a residual remnant of my evangelical upbringing.

Being a minister in The United Methodist Church, with its homophobic church laws, ministering in a local church that is socially conservative, was another part of the struggle. What did it mean for me as a pastor to have a gay son? How would people react if they found out, when they found out?

Moreover, as a parent, you are proud of your child, you want to share important news about your child with the whole world. But I knew I could not share freely, because I feared there would be repercussions. I was becoming more and more aware at that time, too, that The United Methodist Church was taking an increasingly conservative stance toward LGBT rights. So all that was part of my personal struggle.

We never made a public statement about Tim's sexual orientation at the Avon Church. We felt it wasn't our place to do so. It was up to our son to come out if he wanted to. And he did, though not publicly, but he did come out to his youth group leader, his youth group, and to a few other people in church. I remember being amazed at how much support there was for him. Even in this conservative community, my son found support. Obviously, there was also some opposition. But I was especially surprised by some older folks who rallied around him. So that made us hopeful for Tim's future.

ZION OF IONA

NOT LONG AFTER OUR talk with Tim, I felt I needed a break from the local church ministry. I needed to reevaluate my life in light of this new development. I decided to take a year off and enrolled in a chaplaincy residency at the Hershey Medical Center. I talked about it with my district superintendent, Phil Ponce, and was honest with him. I said, "I'm not sure if I'm going back into local church ministry." And I really wasn't sure.

The residency was a good experience for me. My supervisors at Hershey Medical Center as well as my residency group provided me with a good sounding board, and I was able to really talk openly. That was helpful.

Something interesting happened during my time there. As part of the residency, we took different career and personality tests. The results helped me understand that I was called into the parish ministry, after all. I guess, deep down, I knew it already, but the evaluation process confirmed this calling for me. What I struggled with at the hospital was dealing with people suffering from terminal diseases. It was hard for me, because I am a joy-giver. I like to celebrate life and bring hope and inspiration to people. There are not a lot of things to celebrate in the lives of those with terminal illnesses, and it depressed me that there wasn't anything more I could do besides providing a listening presence to patients. So the parish ministry, I discovered, was much better suited for my calling than chaplaincy in a hospital.

So very early on in the program—I'd only been there for three or four months—I let my district superintendent know, "I think I'm going to be open for another church." And that's how I got appointed to the Zion of Iona United Methodist Church.

During the last year of my ministry at the Avon Zion Church, Brigitte and I had built and moved into our own home in Lebanon, Pennsylvania. I indicated to my district superintendent that my family and I would like to remain in the Cedar Crest school district, if possible. This was probably the main reason why I was appointed to another church in Lebanon—which is uncharacteristic for the appointment process of The United Methodist Church. New appointments typically send pastors into another district. My new charge was the Zion of Iona United Methodist Church. There are probably a dozen churches that carry the name "Zion" in the Lebanon area. So I went from the Avon Zion Methodist Church to the Zion of Iona Methodist Church. I served there for more than eleven years, until December 19, 2013. After eleven years of building relationships, friendships, and ministry, I had developed a deep sense of affinity and belonging there.

Zion of Iona is located in the outskirts of Lebanon. It offers ample space inside and out, with a large parking lot and yard space. South Lebanon Township had seen a number of housing developments; it is a growing, thriving community. It is an area that offered good potential for a successful community church ministry. But, more importantly, the people in the congregation were friendly, welcoming, and had a keen sense of the importance of mission.

But I was also under fire at Iona almost from the very first day, because people in the community knew that I had a gay son, and some folks at Zion of Iona took offense to that. In fact, it became an issue even before I started my work at the church, soon after the announcement about my appointment was made. I learned from the Staff-Parish Relations Committee (SPRC) chairperson that there were some congregants who were very concerned about the fact that I had a gay son. Before they even met me, there was already a concern about that. Tim actually didn't attend Zion of Iona regularly, because he left for college just before I started my ministry there. But people knew, and people talked.

So, fires had to be put out even before I started working at the church. I think it was district superintendent Ponce along with the SPRC committee that responded to the concerns, essentially saying: "Look, his son is gay. So what?" And I guess the concerned folks were then willing to give me a chance. When I finally did preach my first sermon and conduct my first service at Zion of Iona, I must have made a good impression on the congregation. I received a lot of positive feedback. When I started, average attendance was around 140, with a membership of around 330. Attendance and membership at Zion of Iona had been higher in the past, but a previous, recent conflict in the church had resulted in the pastoral leadership (a clergy couple) leaving in mid-appointment. A retired minister was sent to the parish as an interim before I was appointed.

Together with a resurgent lay leadership at the church, we were able to bring healing and growth. In fact, we grew too fast for our own good. About a year and a half into my ministry we ran out of room in our Sunday morning worship service, pushing the 200-seat capacity of the sanctuary on a regular basis. Additional chairs were set up in the back of the church and sometimes people actually sat in the coat room. It was a good problem to have, but it was still a problem. Numeric growth is always a result of meaningful ministry; at the Iona church it was the result of new missions we offered to the community, including new children's programs, a senior program, a revived women's program, and a mission team that expanded ministry to the local community.

At around that time, a visionary church leader suggested we should have a ministry audit done. We agreed to proceed and, after going through a process that involved much of the church, we began to implement some of the recommendations from the audit.

One of the first things we had to decide as a church was how to solve the "overcrowding" problem. The audit recommended starting a second service. However, there were some concerns about that, as the church had had a second service in the past that was not successful and was eventually discontinued. So the leadership and I decided that, because of the residual concern, we needed to take a congregational vote. The vote yielded overwhelming support for a second service over the other options of expanding the building or having two services simultaneously.

But even with the congregational vote, there were a few people in the church who were not happy about the second service. There was opposition from the beginning. The chancel choir director, who had served the church for about thirty years at that time, was one of the most outspoken in this regard. As a result, the chancel choir was the only one of the six church choirs that did not sing in the second service. But the second service did resolve the crowding problem and gave us the opportunity to continue to grow as a church.

We also successfully implemented other audit recommendations, such as developing a vision and mission statement: "Connecting people with God's love (in the spirit of John 3:16)." It was an involved process that took another congregational vote to pass. The growing ministry meant we needed additional staff, and we didn't have to look far to fill our newly created pastoral assistant position. Clydette Leone (now Overturf) had already served as our youth director and had taken the hearts of the congregation with her inspirational sermons. Besides her gifts as a youth leader and speaker, Clydette had the educational and leadership skills necessary. We made an exceptional pastoral team, which is part of the reason we continued to expand our ministry and mission into the community via a new small group ministry, an outreach website, and a children's church ministry. A year into the second worship service, the church board voted on another recommendation—to offer a contemporary worship style in contrast to the traditional worship we had in the first service.

On a shoe-string budget, I started a worship band and organized a contemporary service. In many ways it was like starting a new church. In the absence of the choirs, attendance initially dropped. I remember we had to rope off the back pews, so that the small group of thirty to forty people wouldn't look scattered and disconnected in the large sanctuary. Once there was a worship band in place, we created a new praise team director position, which we filled with a talented musician and vocalist. The contemporary service had a humble beginning, but eventually it became so large that we were actually planning a second contemporary service, just before I faced my trial.

It was around the time we started the contemporary service that new tensions began to build. I had always faced opposition and criticism from a small group of traditional-minded folks at the church. These complaints were not untypical of tensions many, if not all, pastors face. Society is changing, and new approaches to ministry are needed to respond to these changes. Paradigm shifts are hard to understand, but they are necessary. For example, today's pastor typically spends less time in the church office and more time on the phone and answering e-mails and FaceBook messages throughout the day, even into the evenings. The trend is that effective pastoral work takes place less at the church and more in the community. But not everybody appreciates these changes, which brings about tensions at times.

However, once the contemporary worship service had established itself, we faced a different problem, the "worship war."

First the tension was underground, but then it bubbled to the surface. Some folks had legitimate concerns; they feared that a contemporary service would diminish the traditional service. We tried to address this concern by keeping the traditional service geared toward the entire family. In fact, I started to advertise the traditional service as the "family service." Others mourned the fact that they could not see everybody on a regular basis on Sunday mornings, as some of their friends were worshiping in "the other" service.

Other concerns were less legitimate. There were some who argued that the contemporary service was against God's will. Others said, "This service will die. It will go away. We tried this before and it failed, and so will this service." Eventually, I was accused of spending more time in preparation for the contemporary service than the traditional one. As a result, some maintained, the performance of the traditional service was declining.

There were also some tensions that had to do with the "kind of people" the contemporary service brought in. The vast majority of the growth in the second service came from community people joining us in worship and ministry, not from the existing membership switching over from the traditional service. The people Clydette and I attracted were on the progressive side, people of different walks, ethnic backgrounds, and sexual orientations.

Our messages of total acceptance, welcome, and unconditional love, grace, and forgiveness reverberated with those folks especially. And the occasional message that alluded to Clydette's and my pro-LGBT rights stance actually drove other, more socially conservative folks away. All this played a part in the complaint against me and the subsequent trial.

TIM'S WEDDING

IN 2006, MY SON TIM called and told me that was going to marry his partner. He'd met Bobby while they were both students at Boston University. Now, at twenty-four years of age, they were ready to make their commitment legal and binding.

"Dad, we would like you to do the wedding. Would you do the wedding for us?" he asked.

And I felt no hesitation at all. It was a no-brainer. My son was getting married. He wanted me to officiate. I knew I wanted to do it. It was an honor and a joy. *Of course* I said, "Yes."

After I got off the phone, I did start thinking about what it might mean for me to perform the wedding. I thought, "All right, I'm doing this wedding. And obviously this is against what it says in The United Methodist Church's *Book of Discipline*." Paragraph 2702 clearly states that a United Methodist minister can be charged and put on trial for performing same-sex marriages. So what was I supposed to do?

I came to the conclusion at the time that I needed to be honest about my plans to preside of my son's wedding to another man, even if it meant losing my job security and my career. I didn't think about the possibility of a trial so much. I just thought that the church would fire me once I made known my participation in a same-sex wedding.

I was fully prepared to lose my job when I entered a written statement in my ministry profile. Every United Methodist minister must submit a ministry profile each year to the bishop and the cabinet. In my profile that year, I wrote:

> I have three children who are gay/lesbian. One of them is living at home. I am affirming gay rights in my theology. It's a social justice issue for me, I have agreed to preside over the marriage ceremony of my gay son, Tim, and his fiancé, Bobby, in April of 2007 (my son resides in Boston, Massachusetts). I have not shared this with anybody in my congregation and do not intend to do so. However, if asked about it, I will not lie.

When I submitted the statement, I thought, "This will probably be the end for me in The United Methodist Church." I knew that in 2005 The United Methodist Church had defrocked a minister named Beth Stroud, for being a "self-avowed, practicing homosexual." It was a long process for Beth, because she had a trial; then the penalty was reversed at the Jurisdictional Council, and she was reinstated. But the counsel for the church appealed the appeal, and the case went all the way up to the Judicial Council—the church's "Supreme Court." And that council upheld the original ruling. So in the end, Beth was defrocked.

During my trial, my written statement to the bishop and the cabinet became a point of contention, as my district superintendent, Rev. Jim Todd, testified that he had not read those portions of my profile and had, therefore, not passed it on to the bishop. I respect Jim's testimony, but I also clearly remember talking to him about Tim and Bobby's wedding.

In fact, I remember him telling me sometime after the wedding that he had "hidden" the "incriminating part" of my profile. I don't know how he hid it (if he did), but the bishop apparently never saw it. If this is what actually happened, I appreciate it, as Jim was being a good pastor and a friend, trying to protect me and keep me in the flock (perhaps thinking it would never become an issue). But at the trial he said he didn't even remember about the wedding. And I can imagine that he really did forget. As a district superintendent, he has had to deal with so many different situations. This combined with the fact that the conversations in question had occurred six or seven years prior to the filing of the complaint against me make this explanation possible.

What makes it even more plausible is the fact that Jim seemed genuinely surprised when I found the evidence of my notifications to the bishop in my personnel file. Jim had allowed me to go through my personnel file as part of my preparation for the trial. My legal team had advised me that I needed to get the evidence straight from my personnel file, because it would contain a stamp that the documents had been received by the district office. Knowing what I was looking for, Jim had previewed my file and told me there was no "smoking gun." But he had looked in the wrong places; perhaps he thought I was looking for the evidence in my annual interview forms. I saw his face when I showed him the "smoking gun," and his surprise was genuine.

I truly appreciated Jim Todd. He was always very pastoral to me, and I consider him a friend. Even throughout the trial he was nothing but supportive and pastoral to me, my family, and my congregation.

I did not make an announcement about Tim's wedding to the congregation of the Iona Church. I had a feeling such an announcement would tear the church apart, given the socially conservative demographics of the congregation as a whole. We were at a growing stage; things were really developing in the church—not just in terms of body count, but also in terms of ministry and outreach. I remember thinking, "Well, this is where I am. I was appointed to this church to be the pastor of these well-meaning people. And yes, they're more conservative than I am, but I have to be faithful to them, as well. I have to think of them where they are and minister to them the best way I can." I just wanted to be the best pastor I could be to the Iona Church and continue to minister in meaningful ways, which also included a subtle education about LGBT inclusion. I felt that this education had to be done through the back door rather than breaking down the front door.

In the end, my fears proved well grounded. When an announcement about my performance of a gay wedding was finally made to the church, it divided the congregation; it turned out to be very painful for everybody involved.

The wedding itself was incredible. It was my first gay wedding, and not just in terms of performing one. I had never even attended a same-sex wedding. The opportunity had never presented itself to me, given the conservative context of my ministry appointment.

I remember thinking, "Okay, what will I do? What will I say? Some things are going to be different."

I thought, "I can't declare them husband and husband. That doesn't sound right, so what do I say? And what changes to I have to make to the liturgy for it to sound authentic?"

I asked advice from my friend Steve Ericson, a minister colleague in Lebanon County who had performed a same-sex marriage ceremony for his daughter. Steve is a United Church of Christ minister, so in many ways his experience was quite different from mine. The United Church of Christ as a whole is open and affirming toward LGBT rights. However, the United Church of Christ is also a congregational church, so each church can decide for itself where it stands on issues. And ministering to a church in socially conservative Lebanon County had consequences for him once his congregation learned about the ceremony he had performed. In the end, he lost a great deal of support and was essentially forced out of his church ministry in Schaefferstown. It was sad to witness things unfold in his church. Of course, Steve had some good pointers for me about the wedding.

Tim's wedding took place on April 28, 2007, in Cohasset, Massachusetts, in a restaurant overlooking the harbor. It was a beautiful place and a beautiful event. About 120 people attended, including some of our extended family, although most of our family in Germany couldn't make it.

Prior to the wedding, I had to get a license in order to perform a legal marriage in Massachusetts. I remember hesitating a bit when I filled out the paperwork registering as a United Methodist minister. I thought, "Is this going to be legal if I perform a marriage in Massachusetts, given the fact that my church opposes same-sex marriage?" At that time, same-sex marriage had been legalized in Massachusetts, but I still had questions about whether it would be legal if a United Methodist minister performed it. After I received the marriage license in the mail, I figured it would be all right.

Only a few people in my church knew about Tim's wedding, and they were people I trusted. I never made a public announcement about it, or even about the fact that Tim was married at all. Tim was not living in Lebanon then, and he had never regularly attended Zion of Iona. He went away to college just before I started my ministry there, and he had not lived in Lebanon since. He came to the church once or twice a year, on Christmas Eve and Easter when he was visiting with us. That was another reason I didn't feel I had to share the news of his marriage—it was a private affair.

In some ways, it was hard not sharing the news. It's not normal to have to hide your child's wedding. It doesn't feel right. It doesn't feel good. At the same time, I was fearful of what an announcement might do and how much discord it could cause. The fear of the potential discord outweighed the pain of not being able to share my son's joy.

But rumors did start circulating about Tim being married, and about whether I had performed the ceremony. And they really started to circulate after our family picture, which included Tim and Bobby, was published in the church's 2008 pictorial directory. It just so happened that our family photo shoot for the directory was scheduled at a time when Tim and Bobby were visiting. We decided to invite Bobby along for the photo shoot. We weren't going to have a picture taken with everybody else and tell him, "You can't be in the picture."

I thought about the decision, of course. In one sense, it was a no-brainer. I mean, there was no question that Bobby would be invited to be in the picture. He was part of our family. But already I could see that it might become a problem. But I said to myself, "Maybe it's no coincidence that Tim and Bobby are visiting when we have a date for the family photo shoot." And looking back, maybe it was meant to be.

I know people talked about our family picture in the church directory, because I heard it through the grapevine. But nobody came to talk with me about it face to face. That's understandable too, I guess. What were they going to say? Most people try to avoid confrontation. So I knew people were talking about it, probably wondering about who this Bobby person was. Was he Tim's husband? It was a safe assumption. And then the question was probably raised, "Did Pastor Frank perform the wedding?"

I'm pretty sure that's how the news about Tim's marriage began to spread through the church. But things didn't come to a head until several years later.

WORSHIP WARS

IN 2012, A NUMBER OF things happened that didn't sit well with a group of conservative members at the Iona Church, the faction that later became known as "the concerned group."

The contemporary service had been the lesser attended service for many years, and while that was the case, some long-time members still held out hope that it would simply go away. But 2012 was a very good year for the second service, in part because of our pastoral assistant, Miles Dissinger, whom we'd hired in 2010. Miles was an excellent praise band leader with a lot of charisma and a great singing voice. Following a series of special events and concerts with our praise band, the contemporary service experienced an explosion in attendance, and we gained many new members. Suddenly, the second service became the bigger service.

In fact, it was getting so big we were actually talking about starting *another* contemporary service. We were having more than 150 people on some Sundays, so it was getting tight in the sanctuary. Miles and I knew we had to do something, and we agreed it was time to start thinking about a third service.

I don't think it is a coincidence that, right around that time, more and more dissatisfaction with the quality of the traditional service was being expressed by members of the concerned group. Some of the expressed concerns were valid, and Miles and I tried to address those. One of those concerns was about keeping the traditional service attractive for children and young families by re-introducing a children's church service, which we were working on. I also incorporated traditional liturgical elements that were said to have been dropped (it must have happened before my time), such as the singing of the *Gloria Patri* and a return to a more "high church" communion liturgy.

I also received criticism over the way eighteen new members were taken in on a Sunday in the fall of 2012. The concern was that there was no confession of faith from any of the new members. I had frequently been criticized on this point, so I knew about the underlying dynamics. Concerned members thought that I made membership too easy; they thought there should have been a more rigorous and selective process in place. But my theology had always been this: If you're willing to join a church in this day and age, you must be in it for the right reasons! I suspect the real dynamic beneath that criticism was a concern over the *kind* of people I was allowing to become voting members of the church. This translated into a concern about the theological direction the church was taking. So it came at no great surprise that this vehement criticism came on the heels of the Iona Church taking into membership on that fall Sunday in 2012 an openly lesbian couple for the first time in its history.

It was around this time that the church's chancel choir director—who had served the church for some forty years—became increasingly uncooperative toward the pastoral leadership. Then, in the spring of 2013, she suggested that she lead the chancel choir in an Easter cantata. Miles and I welcomed the suggestion. However, she wanted to perform the cantata on Easter Sunday, during the traditional service *only*. I told her that having the cantata in only one service would probably draw a number of attendees from the other service and could create a serious seating capacity problem. She eventually agreed to have the cantata for both services.

So I thought we were all set for the special program on Easter Sunday. But just four weeks before the biggest Christian holiday, the day our church was most crowded, I heard through the grapevine that the choir director had canceled the cantata. I immediately called her to find out whether this was true. I had no response until the next Sunday, when I saw her in the hallway of the church. She confirmed that she had canceled the cantata. Of course, the church staff and I hadn't made any other plans for Easter services. The cantata was supposed to *be* the special program. At that point we had to scramble to put a new program together.

I realized then that the chancel choir director had no interest in working with me any longer. I wrote a letter to the church's Staff Parish Relations Committee explaining the communications problems we'd been having with the chancel choir director and concluded, "If she is no longer willing to cooperate and communicate, I want to have you look into the possibility of letting her go."

The committee responded by saying, "We understand the problem. But before we do anything, we want you to talk with her in the presence of a mediator."

Dr. John Schlegel, chairperson of the committee, was willing to act as the mediator. A meeting was scheduled between John, the chancel choir director and her husband, and me.

To say that the meeting did not go well is an understatement. Positive communication just didn't seem possible. In the words of John Schlegel, "It was clear there were irreconcilable differences" between the choir director and me. In the end, the choir director quit. I believe it was a preemptive move on her part. I think she suspected that if she didn't quit, she would be fired.

Although I was saddened that we as confessing Christians could not works things out, I was hopeful that, at least, there would be an end to a conflict that had gone on for most of my eleven years at Zion Iona. Little did I know that this conflict would set in motion a string of events that dramatically changed the life of the church, as well as my own life.

THE FIRST ACCUSATION

THE DAY AFTER THE chancel choir director quit her job, I got a phone call from my district superintendent, Jim Todd. After a short greeting he said, "I hear that you're in a car and that I am on speaker phone. Is there anybody with you in the car?"

I said, "No, why?"

"What I have to say is of a confidential nature. I have to ask you to meet with me right now," he said.

I said, "Jim, I'm on my way to play tennis, and it's a doubles match. If I don't show up, they won't be able to play. It'll take two hours, max."

He said, "Okay, I will meet you right after your tennis match."

When I met with Jim, I learned that an accusation had been made against me—a very nasty accusation. A member of my church at Iona had called the bishop and said I had been caught having sex in the bathroom at the church with a man—our former worship leader. This event had allegedly happened two years prior and had been witnessed by the church janitor.

At the time I didn't know who had made the accusation. Later I found out it was the same man who later filed the complaint against me for performing a same-sex wedding—the son of the choir director who had quit her job just the night before.

My accuser didn't even attend Zion of Iona United Methodist Church at that point. He didn't live in Lebanon. He had been in the military since before I arrived and never attended the church on a regular basis while I was the minister at Zion Iona.

I was stunned.

"Did you do this, Frank?" my district superintendent asked.

"Absolutely not!" I said.

I gave him the church janitor's name and phone number, and had to leave the room while he called her. After pacing in the hall for about ten minutes, I was called back in to the office. Jim said, "The witness said she didn't see anything like this at all. So that's good. But we can't close the matter, because we were told that there's still another witness."

Well, the other witness turned out to be a false witness, a person who simply believed the rumor that this had happened.

And this false witness was responsible for spreading the rumor in the community—not just in the church, but in the outside community. I knew about it because people kept coming up to me and saying, "Do you realize what this man is saying about you?"

Finally, he stopped spreading this awful, baseless rumor. But he was still a member of the church, so I saw him on a regular basis.

My wife and kids were very upset about all of this, of course. One Sunday, Brigitte confronted our false witness in the church hall and said, "Would you please stop spreading this rumor? This is hurting my family."

"Are you threatening me?" he said.

"How am I threatening you?" she answered, genuinely confused.

By this point, the "concerned group" was communicating regularly, so I wasn't surprised to hear that complaints had been made to my district superintendent and the bishop to report that Brigitte had "assaulted" the false witness.

THE "CONCERNED GROUP"

THE CONCERNED GROUP held their first "official" meeting on the Saturday morning before Easter. They called it an emergency church meeting, but they did not include any of the ministerial staff or official church leaders. From what I was told by a participant, there were twenty-five to thirty gathered at a local breakfast place who presented concerns about where the Iona Church was heading under my leadership. Apparently, there was a long list of complaints against me, including the recent conflict with the chancel choir director who had quit. As it turns out, many who gathered in this initial meeting became the "concerned group"—an ad hoc committee I got to experience later as a political action group throughout the rest of my pastorate.

Members of this group soon got behind the same-sex wedding complaint against me, and they remained a political force throughout my eventual trial. Many members of this group were even lined up as witnesses against me in the trial.

Over the next months, members of this group called Bishop Peggy Johnson and my district superintendent, Jim Todd, on a regular basis with complaints and petitions. It seemed as though they were complaining about anything and everything I did, said, and wrote—even my sermon titles. I speculated at one point whether they thought the sheer number of complaints would move the bishop to take action against me, even in the absence of substance.

33

Some members of the concerned group had not been active in worship at the Iona Church for a long time. They had quit coming because they weren't happy about one thing or another in my ministry. Now that there was a chance to get rid of me, they were back with a vengeance.

THE SECOND
ACCUSATION

THE FIRST ACCUSATION died pretty quickly, because it was so obviously a vicious rumor with no grounds in reality. However, going through the investigative process and then facing almost daily complaints from the concerned group, which were always copied to Bishop Johnson and Jim Todd, had an effect on me and my family. I remember asking myself, "If these people keep producing these nasty accusations and complaints without regard to how it affects me or my family, what else are they capable of doing?

I had talked to Brigitte about the possibility of Tim's wedding becoming an issue, but we had dismissed that thought in part because I had actually tried to find the wedding certificate online, but couldn't. And besides, the wedding had happened so many years ago. However, in the back of my mind, there remained an uneasy feeling about that possibility.

Sure enough, about two weeks later I received another phone call from Jim Todd (which, by then, had become an almost daily event), informing me that an official complaint had been filed against me. Unlike the previous accusation, there was evidence for my "offence" in the form of a Massachusetts court transcript of the marriage certificate I had filled out and signed about six years earlier—the marriage certificate of my son's wedding to another man.

Jon Boger, the son of the former chancel choir director, was the official complainant. I still don't know exactly how he got a transcript of the marriage license. I heard from someone I consider a reliable source that Jon and his mother actually drove to Massachusetts to get the document. Boger maintained in a recent e-mail to me that he had simply requested it by mail from the courthouse. Either way, he had the written proof that I had performed Tim's wedding, the marriage certificate complete with my signature on it.

There is a statute of limitations of six years on the charge of performing a same-sex marriage, according to The United Methodist Church's *Book of Discipline*. The official charge was filed twenty-six days before the statute of limitations ran out in my case. The original complaint has some language in it that pointed to the fact that the statute of limitations was close to running out. So Boger was urging Bishop Johnson to act right away to beat the statute of limitations. It seemed like whoever was helping Boger write the complaint had a good grip on the *Discipline*.

I first found out about the official complaint via e-mail from Bishop Johnson. She informed me that a complaint was going to be filed against me, and that was my first heads up. I actually received the complaint by registered mail on April 4, 2013.

I was still serving at the Iona Church, and some of the people who were behind the official complaint were still members. Others had stopped attending services, some of them former choir members, but most of them were part of the concerned group, who decided to boycott the church ministry while I was serving there.

It became obvious to me that the concerned group had narrowed their focus to one goal and one goal only—to get rid of me. A second realization was even more painful: After all these years of caring for many of these people—visiting them when they were sick or in the hospital, working with them, compromising and showing nothing but kindness to them—they actually did not seem to care what happened to me in the realization of their goal. A third realization was equally painful: They didn't seem to care at all about causing pain to my son Tim, or to my family in general. The official complaint filed against me for performing Tim's wedding was simply a cold-hearted means to an end.

REGISTERED JUNK MAIL

WHEN THE COMPLAINT arrived, it came to our house by registered mail. Everything related to the complaint and trial I received after that came by registered mail. One day, my wife started to call it "registered junk mail." I laughed so hard, and that felt good. I so appreciated Brigitte's humor. It was what we needed to survive; it was therapeutic, considering the stress we were put under for committing an act of love and affirmation for our son—an act The United Methodist Church called "a chargeable offense."

Throughout the entire process, almost every day I received registered mail. According to the *Discipline*, all communications between the church and me had to be sent that way, all of the pretrial deliberations, everything. I received a *lot* of registered mail. I remember thinking: "What a waste of resources."

The United Methodist Church's *Book of Discipline* also outlines the procedure that has to be followed when an official complaint is filed. First, there was a meeting between the complainant, the bishop, and the district superintendant. Next, there was a meeting between the bishop, the superintendent, and me.

At the meeting, I was told I was not to contact the complainant at all directly, only through Bishop Johnson. It was almost like a restraining order, an ecclesiastical restraining order. I couldn't contact Mr. Boger in any way. And I didn't.

Boger had his meeting with them first, and he was allowed to bring someone with him. I heard he brought his mother. Immediately after that meeting, I walked into my meeting with Bishop Johnson and Jim Todd, and I could tell from their demeanor that their meeting with Boger had not gone well.

Up to that point, my district superintendant had told me that Bishop Johnson intended to deal with the complaint on an administrative basis and give me an official reprimand. If I accepted a reprimand in my permanent file for having performed the wedding, that would be the end of the case.

But when I walked into that supervisory meeting, all that had changed. Now Bishop Johnson was saying, "I can't handle this matter administratively, because then I would find myself on the bench next to you. And I can help you better if I'm not on the bench next to you." It felt to me as if Bishop Johnson was fearful, as if she had been threatened with consequences if she would not allow my complaint to go to a trial.

"So," she said, "unless a just resolution can be reached between Mr. Boger and you, the matter is going to trial."

I think Bishop Johnson's plan was to handle the trial very swiftly. She said it was her hope and expectation that I would receive a reprimand as a result of the trial. It made sense to me at the time. I remember thinking, "Why would I get any more of a penalty for performing a same-sex marriage for my own son?"

On May 3, 2013, I received a registered letter from Bishop Johnson that had the names of the presiding bishop and the counsel for the church. The trial dates were set for June 24–25, 2013, at a local United Methodist church in Lancaster County, Pennsylvania.

Bishop Johnson and Superintendent Todd also thought it would be best to have a congregational meeting at the Iona Church, during which the entire congregation would be informed about the charges and the trial. We agreed to have a congregational meeting on May 2, with Jim Todd and another district superintendent acting as moderators. While I agreed to the meeting, my heart sank, because I realized that the news about my performing Tim's wedding was going to become public. The wedding, a beautiful family moment for us, would become an issue of debate. And not only was this going to be an embarrassment for our family, I also feared that this kind of controversy had the potential to split the congregation.

INITIAL SUPPORT

AS PLANNED, WE HAD the congregational meeting on May 2, 2013. I remember being worried about it beforehand. But low and behold, that night the vast majority of the people spoke out in support of me—the vast majority. The meeting was well attended, with 160 to 170 in attendance. To my surprise, many seemed upset that the trial was even going to happen, rather than about the fact that I had performed a gay wedding. There were questions like, "Who's the complainant?" The superintendent said he was not at liberty to give out this information. Some expressed disappointment about that.

Members of the concerned group were present, as well. However, only three of them spoke up. The others didn't seem to dare speaking, probably because there was so much support expressed for me. Only three were brave enough to speak.

Even some people who I knew were against gay rights supported me that night. They said things like, "Well, it's his son, after all." Another person said, "If he hadn't done this for his son, not only would I think he's a bad father, but I also could not trust him as a pastor." That was an amazing statement. Again, this was not coming from LGBT supporters. At the conclusion of the meeting, I was allowed to speak. I remember receiving a lot of applause. I left the church more hopeful than I had been in weeks. I wondered that night, "Is this going to be less of a problem than had I first thought?"

On May 6, I received an e-mail from Bishop Johnson that contained a proposal by the complainant, Jon Boger, to enter into negotiations for a "just resolution," which is a process of negotiation to find a solution without a trial. This was surprising, as he initially refused to even offer this process. Boger had not been present at the congregational listening session. But he had doubtless heard about the support I had received. I wondered whether this offer for negotiations had been motivated by that support.

He said in his May 6 proposal that his goal had never been to have the trial become a national event and that he did not want to bring embarrassment to Iona and its members.

Boger's proposal read like this:

I propose the following:

- Enter a letter of censure in Pastor Frank's permanent record of ministerial service that he performed a same-sex union.
- Have him sign a pledge to no longer perform same-sex union ceremonies, unless the United Methodist Church officially changes its position.
- Have him write letter of remorse and repentance to the congregation.

The first and third points I could have agreed to; the second point, however, would have violated my conscience. I knew I could not refuse ministry to anybody based on sexual orientation. And besides, I had two other gay children. What if they asked me to perform their weddings someday?

After seven or eight drafts, I came up with the following counterproposal, which I sent on May 14 to Bishop Johnson to convey to Boger:

To the complainant:

I appreciate the expression of good will in offering reconciliation. After prayerful deliberation and counsel, I have come to the following response:

I am willing to have entered into my permanent record of ministerial service the fact that I performed a same-sex marriage for my son on April 28, 2007.

Love, Frank

My counterproposal was a minimal penalty I was willing to accept. I did not want to give too much in this initial counter, as I assumed a series of counterproposals would follow. To my surprise, Boger decided to stop the negotiations. His response came on May 16:

Dear Bishop Johnson,

Below is my response to Pastor Schaefer's counterproposal for resolution. Since Pastor Schaefer is unwilling to agree that what he did was wrong and refuses to promise "not" to do it again, reconciliation is not possible. Thank you for all your time and I will see you on 24 Jun.

LAWYERING UP

AS JIM TODD WALKED me through the process that was to come, he explained that all parties in the trial were appointed by the bishop. However, the bishop was not responsible for picking a clergy counsel or an attorney for me.

"A clergy council has to be an ordained minister in The United Methodist Church," Jim explained. Then he suggested that I ask Robert Coombe to be my clergy counsel.

I didn't know Bob Coombe, so I went home and looked up his church site online. When I came across his picture, I immediately knew he was someone I wanted on my side. Compassion and grace were written in the features of his face. So I called him up, we met the next day, and he listened to my story. He agreed to be my counsel that same night.

But I still needed an attorney to be the assistant counsel on my team. Rev. Scott Campbell from Massachusetts, who in 2011 defended a United Methodist minister named Amy DeLong in a trial for performing a same-sex marriage, recommended that I contact Attorney William Ewing. Bill had been a long-term member of the progressive Germantown United Methodist Church in Philadelphia. In fact, Bill had been through a church trial of his own, providing counsel to Beth Stroud, an openly lesbian and partnered United Methodist minister who was defrocked in 2005.

In The United Methodist Church judicial system, attorneys are involved, but they remain mostly behind the scenes. The people who do all the talking are ministers. A United Methodist trial calls for the appointment of a bishop to take the role of "presiding officer" (the judge) and the appointment of ordained ministers to the positions of "counsel for the church" (prosecution); "counsel for the respondent" (defense); and a trial court (the jury) made up of thirteen clergy members plus two alternates.

Behind the scenes, attorneys do the majority of the work. They are also present throughout the trial process to advise the bishop and other clergy members who carry out the trial proceedings. The entire trial process is laid out in the *Book of Discipline*, which contains the law code of The United Methodist Church.

The trial was initially scheduled for June. That was one of the first things my counsels appealed. They said, "This is ridiculous. This is all backward."

On May 21, my defense team and I sent a motion to Bishop Johnson. In it we pointed out that, according to the *Discipline*, there first had to be an administrative process, which had already happened. Then, if the bishop finds a matter should be further investigated, he or she must appoint a counsel for the church. The role of the church counsel at that stage is to do an investigation to determine if a trial is warranted. Only then can the bishop set a date and location for a trial. But a trial date had been set before the investigation had even begun, thus making the investigation biased toward what the outcome should be. Not only did we ask Bishop Johnson to rescind the date of the trial, we also asked her to rescind the appointment of the counsel for the church, Dr. Christopher Fisher, as well as that of presiding officer, Bishop Alfred Gwinn, as both, we claimed, were prejudiced by the existing trial date and location.

Just two days later, Bishop Johnson responded by rescinding the trial date as well as the appointment of the presiding officer (though eventually, Bishop Gwinn was reinstated as presiding officer anyway). However, she refused to rescind the appointment of the counsel for the church. So Chris Fisher stayed on as the counsel for the church. He proceeded with the official investigation, after which he concluded there was enough evidence to put me on trial for presiding over the wedding of my son to another man in 2007.

I felt relieved that the trial had been postponed. At that point, it would have been just four weeks away. There would not have been time to prepare for a defense or to raise funds for it. And I felt a defense was not only possible, but entirely necessary since church law (the *Discipline*) contradicts itself. On the one hand, it asks pastors to minister to all people regardless of sexual orientation; on the other, it prohibits ministers from performing a gay marriage, which clearly is a refusal of such a ministry.

A LEAVE OF ABSENCE
AND A MASS DEPARTURE

ONE OF THE FIRST THINGS Bishop Gwinn did as presiding officer was place me under a gag order. For months, I was not permitted to speak about any aspect of the trial, either in public or in my church. Meanwhile, the concerned group bombarded church members with e-mails and phone calls, to which I could not respond. Slowly but surely, they were drawing more people to their side.

Finally, my counsels argued the gag order with the bishop, saying, "Frank has to raise funds for his defense." The church was not paying for my legal expenses, after all. And those expenses were adding up. I already racked up a lot of personal expenses—travel, phone, research, and of course all that registered mail. And there were more significant expenses right around the corner: I would have to pay for transportation and lodging for up to ten witnesses at my trial. I had to raise some funds.

Finally, Bishop Gwinn lifted the gag order, so that I could raise funds for my defense. It was at that time that I began speaking to the press, as well. The case was already receiving a lot of media attention. And of course, reporters were asking me about the wedding for my son and where I stood on my theology concerning gay rights. And I had decided I was not going to lie. Sadly, my honesty eroded some more of my support in the parish. You know, it was one thing for me to perform a single wedding for my son. It was another thing completely for me to be out in the press advocating for gay rights.

I think a lot of my church members thought I was going to say to the trial court, "Well, it was my son, and I did it out of love. But I apologize for doing it, and I'm never going to do it again." A number of my parishioners thought I would basically just ask for forgiveness. But I wasn't going to do that, because that's not what I believe. I couldn't stand before the press and lie about my theology. I had to tell the truth.

So once I started doing press interviews I had to fess up about my theology. People in the church read the interviews, of course, and a number of them began turning away from me because of my inclusive theology on gay rights. It is a fairly conservative church, as I've said, and this issue was controversial. Even some of those who had expressed support for me before began to turn away. During this time, the concerned group managed to come up with more than fifty signatures on a petition to suspend me from my pastoral duties until after the trial.

Before this whole ordeal, I had always assumed that my district superintendent and the bishop were my bosses. But it turns out they had less "power" over me than I thought. Even though people in the concerned group had collected signatures on a petition to suspend me, the church could not suspend me. There was no legal basis for them to suspend me. So the bishop asked me if I would be willing to go on a voluntary leave of absence, fully paid, for three months, beginning on July 1.

I think she felt under pressure and wanted to appease the loud and persistent political faction that was bombarding her and the district superintendent with calls and e-mails. Jim Todd told me at one point, "Most every day we get another communication. You know, we've gotten to the point that we don't even respond anymore."

They were getting a taste of what I had faced at Zion of Iona for many years, because it had gone on for a very long time. I had gone through six or seven crises before the same-sex wedding controversy. And most of the folks in the concerned group had been part of those crises.

A leave actually sounded good to me at the time. I was exhausted from all the drama, the trouble, and the heartbreaks. But my counselors said to me, "Frank, if you do that, if you leave for that long, you're never going to return to that pulpit. That's going to be the end of you at Iona."

Deep down, I knew they were right. Three months is a long time. So, I agreed to take the minimum leave, which was six weeks, beginning on July 1. And then another drama began.

In the preceding months, my assistant pastor, Miles, and I had become concerned over the effect the trial was having on many members of the second service. A lot of them were new to the faith or had returned to the church after long absences. We sensed they were becoming disillusioned with The United Methodist Church. And so we had begun to think about starting our own church, just taking the entire second service and maybe even some people from the first service, and leaving. But then it became clear to me that I couldn't do that, especially if there was still a chance I would simply get a reprimand and be allowed to stay in the church.

But the "exodus group," as it became known later, had continued to meet without me, and they decided they were going to go through with it. They were going to leave The United Methodist Church. And they were going to do it while I was on my leave of absence.

Miles came to me and told me they what they were planning. I said, "Are you serious? You want to leave with a group of people during my leave? Do you know what this is going to do to the church?"

But they were set on doing it right then, in part because they had already rented a place to meet for worship. They were, as I said, disillusioned with The United Methodist Church. They felt that the denominational leadership had empowered a small group at Zion Iona to take the entire church hostage to their agenda, which was causing the ministry to fall apart. They were tremendously upset with what the concerned group had done.

Miles also expressed concern that the concerned group would eventually turn against him. There had been already confrontations, and he was pretty sure the persecution was not going to end with me. So he said, "We have go. And we have to do it now."

So about sixty to seventy people left and began a new church. They took our name, too, the name of the second service. That service was called the Damascus Road service, named after the first Christian contemporary band we had at Zion Iona. The original

Damascus Road band was made up of all youth, and they had led the congregation in a monthly contemporary worship service. So Miles, along with most of the members of our worship band, launched a brand new church fellowship called the Damascus Road Community Church. It is an independent church, not at all affiliated with The United Methodist Church.

Because Miles let me know about the departure before I left, I was able to soften the blow for the church somewhat. We made plans on how to continue the second service without the exodus group and without some of the musicians. And although the group had the blessing of many of us in the church, their departure was still very difficult. For one thing, it gave additional ammunition to the concern group, who claimed that the exodus group was leaving because of my lack of leadership, although Miles had been very clear in a letter to the congregation that this was not the case.

Many of the people who remained at Zion Iona were devastated, especially those who had attended the contemporary service. Some perceived the group's departure as an abandonment, others as a betrayal. I tried to tell them, "Well, you know, there's another side. They were concerned for some of the people who are new to the faith, because of all that's happening at the church." But a lot of people struggled with it, and there were some additional tensions at Zion Iona for a while.

Because of the departure of the exodus group, I also had a legitimate reason to cut short my leave of absence: I had to get involved with the logistics of the separation. Also, I had to come back early to lead the worship, which I had not done regularly since Miles had become our worship leader. The contemporary service had to continue. We had worked too hard, for too many years, to give up.

RAISING DEFENSE FUNDS

MY SUPPORTERS AND I DECIDED that a good way to raise money for my defense would be to hold a benefit concert. Chaz DePaolo, a New York Hall-of-Fame rock and blues artist who was also a good friend of mine, had originally suggested it to me. Jimmy Creech, the first pastor ever defrocked by The United Methodist Church for performing a same-sex wedding, agreed to give the keynote address that night. I felt so honored, and was very much looking forward to meeting Jimmy in person.

The concert was set to take place on September 29 and was directed by a dear friend, Rev. Shellie Sterner, a United Methodist minister who was on a leave from ministry at the time. Shellie was the only United Methodist minister in Lebanon County who not only stood behind me but also beside me. There are more than thirty churches in the county, but no other local ministers publicly stood beside me. If it had not been for Shellie's support, I would have felt very isolated. She stood by our family's side through all the new and challenging experiences that lay ahead. And she quickly found others in the community to help with the benefit concert.

The local LGBT group at Lebanon Valley College helped tremendously. In fact, they asked the college if we could hold the concert there. It would have been a free venue. But the leadership at the college dragged their feet on it and referred the request to the college's board of trustees. The trustees decided it was just too controversial. They didn't want to have the concert at the college. We also asked a couple different churches in the community to host it, with no luck. There were some churches willing to host it in Lancaster or Lancaster County, but it was important to us to have the concert in Lebanon.

So we ended up having it at the Expo Center in Lebanon, which was a neutral place. It was a little pricey, but it all worked out in the end. I'm not even sure how much money we raised. I think at the concert, after all expenses, we raised close to $2,500. Even after the concert, funds came in via a community Facebook page my son Tim had started entitled, "Stand With Frank: Support Equality." That Facebook page really took off. Altogether, it went to around 15,000 likes during that period. It was amazing how quickly the news of the trial spread.

We also had a candlelight vigil, which was organized by a growing group of local Lebanon supporters, such as Marcus Sprecher, Sirae Sprecher, Joy Riley, and Vanessa Marinkov. Some of them were old friends, some of them new. Each had a story that connected them with the LGBT community. None of them were members of my church. I could have easily asked people for help at Zion Iona, and I'm sure the majority of them would gladly have accepted, but I felt constrained by the concerned group, who would have made this another "scathing point" on their list of criticisms. Every message we put out on the Facebook page, every tweet, and every interview I gave was reported to Bishop Johnson and Superintendent Todd, and links were e-mailed to members of the congregation.

The priest of an Episcopal church in Lebanon offered his church for the local candlelight vigil. However, once it was announced in the *Lebanon Daily News*, members of his congregation brought it up as a concern in a council meeting, after which we were asked not to hold the event there. The reason given by the council: "We shouldn't get involved in the controversy of another denomination." In the end, we held the vigil at Coleman Chapel, a little wedding chapel on Rt. 422.

The candlelight vigil was not simply a local event. An appeal went out to different churches and organizations around the country to hold their own candlelight vigils for me and my family. We put out some advertisements, even a video and materials churches could download, such as flyers and church bulletin inserts. And we heard about a good number of candlelight vigils that were organized just a week before the trial began.

Matt Berryman, executive director of Reconciling Ministries Network (RMN)—an independent progressive caucus working within The United Methodist Church—had reached out to me shortly after judicial charges were filed against me in July. Being an ordained Methodist pastor himself, he had tremendous insights that helped me understand the dynamics of my situation. He was a great source of encouragement. When he contacted me, just ahead of the 2013 RMN Convocation "ChurchQuake" in early September, he encouraged me to have the trial announced there. He said this announcement would have the potential to rally support behind me. I trusted Matt's assessment and agreed, although I asked him to not mention any details of the trial, as at that point I was still under the gag order. Matt was right; as a result of the announcement, I was contacted by dozens of folks, pledging their support.

The benefit concert on September 29, 2013, was the first time the story hit the local TV news. I had been interviewed by newspaper reporters right after the gag order was lifted. In mid-September I talked to the *Lebanon Daily News*, then to the *Patriot News* of Harrisburg. From there the story spread to the *Philadelphia Inquirer*, and then it became more of a regional story. It was also picked up by the *Huffington Post*.

But the concert marked the first televised coverage the case received. The night of the concert, a news team from Channel 8, a local NBC affiliate, showed up…and we very nearly sent them away by mistake. We had a group providing security for the concert, in case protesters showed up. One man on the security team saw the Channel 8 van coming and he sent them away. He said, "No press."

But he had gotten the reporter's business card, so we called him right back. Chris Hush of Channel 8 News was very understanding and did an excellent job reporting on the benefit concert and the reason behind it.

Then I started getting phone calls from more news stations in the area—the ABC and CBS and Fox News affiliates. I started to do interviews in the church office, and that became another point of contention for the concerned group, of course.

Another publicity boost came on November 9, 2013, just a couple of weeks before my trial. That day, thirty-six United Methodist ministers from Bishop Johnson's episcopal area (plus a dozen more ministers from other denominations) jointly performed a wedding for Richard Taylor and William Gatewood at Arch Street United Methodist Church in Philadelphia. I had been invited to speak at a meeting just the week prior, so I got to spend some time with these wonderful colleagues who put their jobs on the line to stand in solidarity with me. The Reconciling United Methodists of the Eastern Pennsylvania Conference had sponsored the event, which was modeled after a similar mass-clergy same-sex marriage ceremony that took place in California more than a decade before.

This show of solidarity was such a boost to our moral! Here were a sizeable number of colleagues who stood behind me and with me, declaring the exclusive policies of the church unbiblical and discriminatory. This ceremony really fueled debate within The United Methodist Church and also got the attention of the media.

But the ceremony was not really about me, of course. It was about Rick and Bill, the couple who got married. They had been together for more than twenty years. When they got wind about the planned mass ceremony, they immediately said, "We want to be the couple." They wanted to make a statement to the world and support me, too.

I attended that wedding at Arch Street, led by the church's senior pastor, Rev. Robin Hynicka. It was a beautiful and moving ceremony, well attended and well spirited. I felt like I was part of an historic moment when Pastor Robin proclaimed, "This day marks a new beginning for The United Methodist Church." After all, I knew from my own gay children that sexual orientation is not a choice for people, and there was no doubt in my mind that all of us, including my brothers and sisters and my clergy colleagues who gathered at the Arch Street service, were on the side of God's love and grace. I left the church more hopeful for the future, feeling that we were on the right side of history and that, one day soon, the persecution of LGBT persons would stop and the church would once again welcome and affirm all of God's children.

ON THE HOME FRONT

DURING ALL THIS TIME, my family was dealing with a lot of emotions, a lot of mixed feelings. In all the years before the complaint was filed against me, I felt I couldn't really talk openly about the issue of homosexuality in the church, or even let people know officially that Tim was gay or that I had performed his wedding. I couldn't officially take a stand for my own children, or for the LGBT community in general. Over the years, I had preached three or four sermons in which I mentioned the issue. And every single time that happened, I got a strong reaction. On two occasions, people actually left the church and let me know they left because of some statement I had made about homosexuality that they thought was contrary to biblical teachings. It was that bad. So I did what I thought I could get away with, and that was to preach on the unconditional love of God, God's grace and forgiveness, and the fact that God accepts all of God's children and so should we. Over the years, I received serious requests for sermons about hell, God's judgment, and condemnation; every time I started preaching on those topics, I ended up on love and grace anyway. I just wasn't cut out to be a "hellfire and brimstone" preacher.

The fact that almost everybody in church knew that I had gay children, coupled with a ministry of love and acceptance of all, in fact, opened the door for a good diversity of people from the community, many of whom started to worship at Zion of Iona. A small number of those were gay and lesbian.

So for me, and also for my family, we felt good about finally being able to be open and to let people know what we really believed about gay rights. It felt good to finally say out loud that The United Methodist Church's position on homosexuality was wrong, that it was discrimination, and that it was harming people, as it had my son. So that felt good. My kids and my wife kept telling me they were proud of me for finally taking a stand and coming out on my beliefs. And it was a coming out, in a sense, for me, because we are an LGBT family, and I'd never felt free to talk about it. So now I was able to do that, and it was a freeing experience.

And we did get a lot of support, which was another thing we felt good about. We were finally able to connect to the larger LGBT community and its allies. As news about the trial spread, support poured out over us from people we didn't even know, much of it from churches that were open and affirming toward the LGBT community. People wrote letters, notes, and e-mails, which encouraged us tremendously. The local support we got was amazing as well, so all of that helped and encouraged us.

But then, of course, there was also the bad stuff. Even in the pretrial deliberations, I was being continually frustrated. First, I wasn't allowed to do this, then I wasn't allowed to do that. It was just one thing after another. I really was stripped of a lot of rights I thought I had. This was definitely *not* going to be my day in court, because I couldn't actually argue what I wanted to argue. It was very frustrating.

There was also so much happening in the church that was hurtful and stressful. We felt the effects of all the turmoil and the constant bombardment of criticism. I actually felt unsafe at one point. I remember thinking, "If they are willing to do all this, where are they going to stop? I felt terrorized, because the attacks were relentless.

It was very difficult to continue in my ministry. It's hard to sincerely preach on love and forgiveness while you're under constant unjust attack that leaves you hurting inside. I needed to constantly work on what I preached—to forgive those whom I felt were unjustly attacking me and trying to destroy my ministry and my career. Before the start of each service, I would pray and try to reach a higher mental state—a state of oneness with God and inner peace. I constantly reminded myself how Christ prayed for his enemies when they put him through torture and nailed him to the cross: "Father, forgive them, for they know not what they do." It became my prayer for those whom I felt were persecuting me. And it really helped put things into perspective for me; after all, at least I wasn't being nailed to a cross!

Throughout this time I still needed to be a minister to all, even to those who attacked me. I was still called to minister to them. On one occasion, I even had to mediate between a leader from the concerned group and the part of the congregation that was supportive of me. I had heard that one of the concerned group members said he didn't feel safe coming to worship at Zion of Iona because some people had confronted him on actions that he felt were his rightful duty as a concerned parishioner. I remember calling him and proposing that we make a joint statement to the congregation, which we did the very next Sunday. We proclaimed that although we might disagree on theological issues, we still respected and accepted one another as fellow Christians. We then deliberately hugged in front of the congregation. I received positive feedback from several members of the concerned group following that action. It made me hopeful that things would change, but my hopes were dashed pretty quickly, as the attacks continued.

Our youngest son, Pascal, was there for part of it. He graduated in May from high school and moved away to college in August. Thankfully, he didn't encounter any trouble his last weeks at high school, because at that point news of the trial wasn't out in the community yet. And he had actually chosen not to come to church anymore, because of all the things that were happening there. And that was probably a good thing. It was that bad.

But the good aspect for my kids was that now, finally, Dad was talking. That had been a point of contention, to be honest—not between my children and me, but between my wife and me. Brigitte had always tried to pushed me, saying things like, "Look, why don't you mention more about equal rights? Why don't you make clearer statements on where you stand theologically?" We'd even had a bit of an argument about her putting an equality sticker on her car. She said, "It's my car. It's not your car." And she did put the sticker on, over my objections.

It's hard to be a pastor's spouse, and it was especially hard in those months leading up to the trial. In fact, it got to the point where Brigitte said to me, "You know what? I'm going to start going to another church. I want to go to a church that's open and affirming, because I can't live like this. This is ridiculous." So she always challenged me to do more and to say more.

Brigitte was completely supportive of me finally taking a stand. But, of course, all of the problems in the church took a toll on her, too. And they took a toll on my children. If something like that happens to you as a family, of course, everybody talks about it in the family. A lot of conversations in our house started with, "Did you hear the latest?" There was so much drama and so much trauma. But this was, in many ways, only the beginning.

MEANWHILE, BACK
AT THE CHURCH

DURING ALL THIS TIME, I was still working full-time at the church. I knew I had to do something to rescue the second service, after the departure of so many of its members. We also had to hire someone to replace Miles.

Years earlier, we'd had an assistant pastor named Clydette Leone Overturf. She had worked alongside me for many years. Then she felt called into counseling and moved out of state. Now she was back in eastern Pennsylvania, and she had indicated about a year prior to the pretrial phase that she would love to come back to Zion of Iona if there was an opening.

People at the church had always loved and appreciated Clydette's ministry. I decided the best thing I could do for the church was to bring her back. Especially with her background in counseling, it seemed like the perfect plan. The SPRC agreed in a unanimous decision, and we hired Clydette back as our pastoral assistant.

Of course, many folks in the concerned group were unhappy about that. They didn't want Clydette. They argued there was no money in the budget to hire an assistant pastor. And truthfully, the church was having a hard time financially. With the departure of the exodus group on the one hand, and the concerned group withholding their pledges on the other, the church was in bad shape financially. But the SPRC hired Clydette anyway. And that decision would prove to be redemptive, as she held the church together throughout a trial that took me out of the church abruptly.

The concerned group continued to cause trouble during the time before my trial. Some of these people were still on church committees; interestingly, they showed up for the meetings, although many of them refused to come to worship.

At one administrative council meeting, one of them said, "Well, we have a problem. We have to take out a loan just to pay our bills. And we really have to take out like $40,000, because we have already dipped into other funds and we can't do that, that's illegal. These are designated funds, and we have to keep the cash for those funds on hand at all times."

The administrative council decided that we would not take out a loan of $40,000 to replenish all the funds; instead, we would borrow only $12,000, just to pay the bills that we had to pay.

The very next day, another member and leader of the concerned group who wasn't even at the meeting called Superintendent Todd and left a message on his phone. He said he was giving a courtesy "heads up" to the district superintendent because he was going to call the police, the township police, to charge the church with "theft of funds."

So I got another call from Superintendent Todd... What else was new? He told me what was going on. After I explained how we had handled church funds, the superintendent assured me that we had done nothing illegal.

But then he said, "Well, this man seemed very upset, and he will probably call the police. I will try to talk him down, but in case I don't succeed, I want you to preempt his call by calling the township police yourself to warn them there might be an accusation about a 'theft of funds.'"

This was, by far, one of the most awkward phone conversations I have ever had. The police officer I spoke with said, "Wait, you've got to back this up. Don't you have a supervisor? Isn't something like this handled internally by the church?"

I replied, "Yes, I do have a supervisor. And I've talked with him about it, and he told me to call the police. Because this disgruntled church member has threatened to call the police, I needed to let you know up front that our books are all in order, and they are totally open, if there's any question. We have nothing to hide."

This is the kind of stuff that was going on behind the scenes at the church in those days. There was always something else, something new, some new accusation, some new negative statement, or a complaint or threat of an action of some sort. It definitely took an immense toll on the church and its members.

PREPARING FOR
THE TRIAL

I TOOK A TWO-WEEK vacation before the trial began to prepare myself, because there was a lot of work to do. People have no idea how much work a trial is, even if it's just a church trial. It's amazing.

The pretrial deliberations alone are a huge undertaking. Basically, you have the trial before you have the trial. Long before the actual trial event, the judge is asked to make a number of rulings about what will be allowed at the trial. We got a lot of registered letters saying, "Well, we'll allow this, but not that." There was a constant flurry of motions and countermotions, statements and objections that went back and forth between the counsel for the church, the judge, and our defense team. We raised objections to what the counsel for the church was proposing. And then he had the right to object to what we had objected to, to argue why this should be allowed or not allowed. It was a long and frustrating process.

The pretrial period started with the judicial complaint being filed in early July. So from early July right up until the trial, there were all kinds of deliberations. And all these communications were sent by registered mail in addition to e-mail.

We had to submit a list of witnesses, along with a description of what each one was going to testify about in the first phase of the trial. The first phase was the guilt-or-innocence phase, and that was a separate phase from the penalty phase. The other side would raise objections to our witnesses, and we raised objections to theirs. It went back and forth like that for a while.

First of all, the church counsel wanted about a dozen people from the Iona Church as character witnesses against me. All of them were members of the concerned group. Some of these folks had not even been in the church for years. So we raised objections about that, of course. But they also raised objections about our witnesses. And then the judge wanted to know more information. What *exactly* was each witness going to testify about? Basically, the judge wanted the testimony before the official testimony was given in court.

So then we had to go back to our witnesses, and we had to coach some of them, and we had to come up with more extensive descriptions of their testimony.

And, in the end, it was all for nothing, because the judge decided he would not allow *any* of our witnesses from the Iona church in the first phase of the trial—the guilt/innocence phase. The only witnesses allowed were to be me and Jon Boger, the complainant.

But the judge would also not allow any of my expert witnesses during the innocence/guilty phase of the trial. This was in part because he had ruled that I wasn't allowed to argue with one portion of the *Discipline* against another. After all, he argued, it is not the *Discipline* that is on trial here.

But this had been the plan for my defense from the start. I wanted to claim that I *was* faithful to the *Discipline* and obedient to the church because I ministered to *everybody*, just as the *Discipline* says in Article IV ("Inclusiveness of the Church") that a minister is charged to minister to everybody, regardless of gender, nationality, race, socioeconomic status.

I was faithful to that part of the *Discipline*, over against paragraph 2702, which says a minister is not supposed to perform a gay marriage. But I wasn't allowed to make that argument. It was all ruled out of order. None of our arguments would be allowed at all. None of our expert witnesses would be allowed, including our "star witness," Dr. Thomas Frank. The only thing, it seemed, I was allowed to witness to in that first phase was, "I performed the wedding for my son." Period. How is that a defense?

I was actually facing two judicial charges. The first was that I had performed a same-sex marriage. And it was pretty clear to all of us that I was going to be found guilty of that. I pled not guilty on this charge. My reasoning on that was this: If I said, "I'm guilty of it," I would be acknowledging that the law was right and not discriminatory. But to me the law itself was discriminatory. So I refused to plead guilty to this first charge.

What I had hoped to do in the trial was to put the discriminatory parts of the Discipline on trial. That was the defense's plan, but as I said, it was thwarted by the church counsel and the judge.

The second charge was that I violated the order and the discipline of The United Methodist Church—not the *Book of Discipline*, but the entire order and discipline of the church. We thought that I would be found "not guilty" on that count. For that purpose we wanted to bring into the witness stand Thomas Frank, who is the foremost renowned scholar on the *Book of Discipline*, admittedly so. Had Dr. Frank been allowed to testify in the guilt/innocence phase of the trial, the outcome might have been different.

While Dr. Frank was not allowed to testify on the first day of the trial, he was allowed to do so on the second day, for the second phase of the trial—when the court had to deliberate on an appropriate penalty for me.

Dr. Frank's argument was beautifully done. In effect, he said, "Look, The United Methodist Church is a big tent. We are a diverse people with diverse opinions and convictions. And, of course, we differ on this issue, on homosexuality. And that's the reason why you find so many contradictory statements in our *Book of Discipline*. It's because it reflects the diversity that we represent as a United Methodist people." His argument was that I was faithful to some parts of the *Discipline* when I performed Tim's wedding.

He also argued that you couldn't judge a minister based on *one* action when it came to the second charge, the charge of having violated the order and discipline of the entire United Methodist Church.

The judge was a retired bishop from North Carolina named Alfred Gwinn. We knew going into the trial that he was fairly conservative.

Bishop Gwinn had been appointed by Bishop Johnson to be the presiding officer at the original trial date. Following the defense's motion to delay the trial, Bishop Johnson rescinded the appointment of Bishop Gwinn and, after judicial charges were filed, appointed another bishop, Warner Brown, from the California-Nevada Annual Conference. Bishop Brown is from the Western jurisdiction, where complaints about LGBT issues do not get to trials very often; even if they do, the penalties are minimal.

In fact, just recently Bishop Hagia from the Western jurisdiction dealt with two such complaints against two pastors in his conference administratively, by giving each of them a 24-hour suspension. Neither case went to trial.

But Bishop Warner recused himself after about a week. I often wondered if my trial would have had a different outcome had he been the presiding judge. The next thing we knew, Bishop Johnson had reappointed Bishop Gwinn.

Bishop Gwinn not only disallowed any witnesses during the first phase of my trial, he also didn't allow any of my exhibits. And there was evidence. We had the profile forms that contained my statements to the bishop and the cabinet, informing them of my intent to perform Tim's wedding.

This form, along with the one that briefly stated that I had celebrated Tim's wedding, was in my personnel file. I made an appointment with my district superintendent to look through my file before the trial. And I found both forms in my district file, both the one I wrote before and the one I wrote after the wedding. I had the district secretary copy them for me. Both had been stamped "Received," with the date on which they had been received. I had both of them in hand, with the stamps indicating they had been received.

But Bishop Gwinn would not allow them in as evidence. That became an issue for me during the trial. On the first day, I was allowed to mention that I had informed my superiors about the wedding in writing. And that prompted a question from one of the jury members, not once, but twice: "Is there any physical evidence of this written statement he made to the district supervisor?" the jury member asked. And still Bishop Gwinn wouldn't allow the evidence in. It could have made a difference.

Another thing that made it difficult in terms of the witnesses was this: The bishop didn't allow any witnesses during the first phase, but he also said, "I will not allow any witnesses for the second phase, because I don't know whether there's going to be a second phase." Because, of course, had I been acquitted, there would have been no second phase. But this made planning for witnesses very difficult. For example, we ended up booking Dr. Frank's flight the night before the penalty phase, which made it quite expensive, of course.

During the pretrial phase, I was still working full-time at the church. That's why I took a vacation two weeks prior to the trial, because the preparations became so overwhelming. I knew the last two weeks were going to be the home stretch, because a lot of preparations came down to the last two weeks. During that time, in addition to everything else, we also had to come up with questions and a procedure for the trial court pool, the jury pool. What kind of questions were we going to ask them? How would we proceed in selecting the thirteen jurors and the two alternates?

I preached my last sermon before the trial at Zion of Iona on November 3, and I remember wondering if it would be the last sermon I would ever preach there. The thought filled me with a sense of deep sadness. I felt the sermon needed to be on choosing love as the high road, even if your enemies hate you and want to destroy you. I didn't have to look far for help with that topic. During my darkest times, I had often looked for inspiration to one of my biggest faith heroes, Dr. Martin King, Jr. In fact, I chose to rework one of my favorite sermons of his, entitled "Love Your Enemies," and incorporate it into my sermon on that day. I concluded my sermon with an extensive quote from his sermon:

> There is a power in love that our world has not discovered yet. Jesus discovered it centuries ago. But most men and most women never discover it. For they believe in an eye for an eye and a tooth for a tooth; they believe in hating for hating; but Jesus comes to us and says, "That's not the way."
>
> So this morning, as I am addressing all those out there who consider me an enemy, I say to you, "I love you! And I will never do you harm. I would rather die than hate you."
>
> And I believe with all my heart that through the power of this love that Christ is teaching us, even some people that choose to hate will be transformed. We will be able to change the world with the redemptive power of love that reaches out even to our enemies, and that blesses those who curse us.
>
> —Dr. Martin Luther King, Jr., from his sermon,
> "Love Your Enemies"

THE TRIAL, DAY ONE

THE TRIAL TOOK PLACE at Camp Innabah, near Spring City, Pennsylvania, about an hour and fifteen minutes from where I lived in Lebanon. It's fairly accessible, a short drive. I probably could have commuted, but I stayed at the camp because we had so much work to do. My counsels and I stayed up until one or two o'clock in the morning to finish the opening statements, closing statements, and defense strategies.

Camp Innabah is a beautiful place. My children attended the camp when they were just kids. My son Tim, who would have to testify at my trial, mentioned how odd it was to be back in that place that held such happy memories for him, and to be there under such different and difficult circumstances. It was a very emotional experience for him.

The trial began on November 18. I went up the day before because we had a pretrial meeting with everybody involved. Jon Boger, the complainant, was part of that meeting, as well.

I had met Boger before. I had baptized one of his children and I had recently performed his grandfather's funeral. I knew who he was. I had talked to him off and on when he came to church. But I didn't really know him, personally. I shook his hand at that meeting and remember feeling absolutely no disdain for him, despite all the ugly stuff, all the false accusations and hardships he had heaped upon me and my family. But perhaps that wasn't too much of a surprise, as I had never held any kind of grudge against him before. I think I saw him as a person loyal to his family—in this case, his mother. The issue between us wasn't personal.

They had converted the camp gymnasium into a makeshift courtroom. It's a relatively new gymnasium, and they had designated all the seats for the presiding officer and the jurors, the counsel for the church on one side and the counsel for the defense on the other. We both had a group of chairs behind us. Each side could have ten people in a special section, family members and supporters, witnesses, and so forth.

Spectators were also allowed in, but they only set up about 120 chairs, 150 at the most. There was a lot of unused space, but the judge limited seating to that amount, and they actually gave out tickets for spectators. When the tickets were gone, people were turned away. There were actually a lot more people who wanted to attend the trial, but couldn't.

There was media coverage ahead of time. But cameras weren't allowed in the room. Journalists and reporters were allowed to sit in the room without using any kind of electronic devices. They allotted four spaces for United Methodist-related media and only four spaces for mainstream media. There were about thirty reporters, many with TV or photo cameras just hanging around outside or in a special room that had no coverage of the trial.

Every time there was a break or we walked out of the building, a whole barrage of cameras got stuck in my face. And I couldn't say a thing, because during the trial I was under a gag order again. I remember saying, "Thank you for coming. I can't talk to you. I can't make a statement. Sorry about that." The news media were able to interview people who weren't part of the trial, but mostly, they just hung out in the press room. Some reporters were actually there for the duration of the trial. I remember feeling sorry for them.

Anticipating a possible attack on my person, Clydette's husband, Ben Overturf, an Iraq war veteran, had asked if he could be my body guard. I had to laugh at first, but when Ben's face remained serious, I started to think maybe that wasn't such a bad idea. So I was privileged to have my first body guard ever, and it actually felt good to have him by my side, not because I was actually facing attackers but because there seemed to be a constant sea of people around me, often blocking my way.

Anticipating the Church's unfriendly attitude toward the press (because of the pretrial deliberations), I talked to RMN about what could be done to keep the trial public. They suggested providing a flow of information from around the trial as well as updates from the trial during breaks. RMN's Andy Oliver, a PR and communications "guru," was put in charge of operation "public trial." To this day I have no idea how he provided a constant stream of information from the courtroom to the press room, but somehow there was a constant stream of tweets going out, as well as minute-by-minute blog updates in the *Lebanon Daily News* and the *Washington Post*, among others.

Just as in a civil trial, seating the jury was the first order of business. We had four random objections we could use for whatever reason—we don't like the beard, whatever—no questions asked. And the counsel for the church had four random objections as well. But there were also questions we could ask and questions they could ask. All of the questions had to be approved by the judge beforehand.

The jurors were all from the Eastern Pennsylvania Conference. Although the *Discipline* allows for elders from other conferences, all of our jurors ended up being from my episcopal area.

My defense team and I became a bit upset during the jury selection. All of the potential jurors were asked this question: "Can you be objective in this case?" Two potential jurors said in response, "No, I can't be objective. He did it. He's guilty." So you'd think those two would have been immediately dismissed from serving on the jury.

Instead, it seemed as if the counsel for the church and the judge did their darned best to keep those people on the jury. They kept asking different questions. "Well, let me put it this way, can you hear new evidence that's presented here?" It was ridiculous. These two people said from the start, "I'm biased and I shouldn't be here." Yet both of them were put on the jury.

We didn't know how long the first phase of the trial was going to take. We thought it might be over quite soon, because originally all I was going to be allowed to say on the witness stand was, "Yes, I did the wedding." So, going into the trial knowing that I was limited in what I could do in terms of putting up a defense on the first day, we came up with a plan.

The plan was this: I had a whole speech prepared that I was going to recite from memory. I had it all lined out on paper. After I said, "Yes, I did it," at a time before the bishop sent the jurors off to deliberate, I was supposed to jump up out of my seat and start delivering this speech. And then, of course, we thought I would be stopped. The plan was that my clergy counsel, Bob Coombe, would then jump up and say, "He's exercising his right according to *Discipline* paragraph 2701.2a ("In any judicial proceedings, the respondent [the person to whom the procedure is being applied] shall have a right to be heard before final action is taken"). Are you refusing the respondent his right to be heard?"

So that was the original plan. But everything kept changing, right up to the last minute. Given that fluid situation, we couldn't be as well-prepared as we needed to be in the courtroom. Thank God we had smart and experienced consultants with us, most notably Dr. Thomas Frank, Scott Campbell (Amy DeLong's counsel), Danny Williams (Beth Stroud's counsel), Kevin Nelson, Dr. Paul Fullmer, and Janet Wolf. Tom Frank and Janet Wolf were also expert witnesses.

I remember being so inspired and encouraged by my attorney, Bill Ewing, whose experience showed when he coordinated the team and delegated different parts and responsibilities. You see, our consultants were close by; they were right behind our table in the reserved seating area for the defense. We often consulted with them during court recesses, and notes were passed even during the proceedings. Most importantly, they were writing different parts of the opening and closing statements, four in all. I don't know how we could have done without them, for as the trial proceedings took interesting twists and turns, our strategy and statements kept changing. There was little you could do to be prepared ahead of time, even though we tried to be. It was kind of humorous to see my clergy counsel, Bob Coombe, reading his closing statements from sheets of paper and iPads that were prepared by different people from our team. But you would have never known it just listening to him. The delivery of his statements was coherent, compelling, passionate, and moving.

So, right before I went into the courtroom on the first day, William Ewing, my attorney, came up with a brilliant idea. It was a last-minute change in strategy.

He said, "Why don't we try this? When Frank takes the stand, Bob, why don't you ask questions about him that have nothing to do with this case? Let's try to make him more human to the jury. Ask questions about his family, about how he came to the ministry, about his ministry at the church before all of the controversy started. Let's make him look like just one of the colleagues." Until Bill made this suggestion, it had not even occurred to me that the thirteen jurors would not know me personally; that it would, in fact, be grounds for recusal for any of them had they known me personally.

Bill continued to explain, "Frank, you just continue into the story of your son, and maybe you'll get that in, maybe they won't stop you. You'll never know until you try."

And sure enough, that's exactly what happened. I got to tell my whole story in court. I was able to tell the story of my son, about the anonymous phone call, about Tim's struggle with the church and how we affirmed him. I felt like I was able to put in a whole defense, and they never stopped me. Even though, according to the pretrial deliberations, I wasn't allowed to present any of this in the first phase of the trial. I still wonder to this day how this was possible. I can't come up with an explanation other than people were drawn into the story, and by the time the church counsel and judge realized what was going on, the truth of our experience was out.

There were so many sidebar talks at the judge's table. I think it was indicative of the fact that none of the participants was very experienced in church trials. I actually got to like the sidebars; I experienced them as bonding moments. It seemed like the participants became less concerned about our differences in opinion and more about the trial process. Perhaps that would have been different if the complainant and his counsel, who was the vice president of the Good News movement (a very conservative and outspokenly anti-gay rights caucus in The United Methodist Church), had been part of the sidebar discussion. Fortunately, they weren't.

There was one surprising moment during one of the first sidebar discussions, when the judge reversed his pretrial ruling that prevented me from saying in court that I had written evidence that I had informed my superiors about my performance of the same-sex wedding for my son. The prohibition was lifted because of something Jon Boger said in his testimony.

Boger's testimony was basically that he was an officer in the Navy. As a military officer, he had taken a vow to serve his country. Because of that service, he had missed many important events in his children's lives. So he understood where I was coming from, that I loved my son and wanted to do things for him. But, he said, I too had taken a vow, to minister and uphold the *Discipline*, and I hadn't kept my promise.

When my counsel cross-examined Boger, he asked about the conflict in the church, about Boger's mother, the choir director. "Isn't it true that just prior to you filing the complaint your mother had been separated from the choir ministry after forty years at the church? So would you say that the complaint you filed is connected to this internal personnel issue? Is this a vendetta?"

Boger said there was no connection. He claimed it just so happened he'd found out about the same-sex wedding I had performed at around that time. And it upset him so much that he felt compelled to file this complaint.

He also testified that his complaint was not really about bigotry or discrimination. After all, he said, he had gay people who worked under him in the military and he respected them. It was weird, because on one hand he was so upset that I had performed my son's same-sex marriage that he had to file a complaint; but on the other hand, he didn't want to appear as a homophobe. And he definitely didn't want to acknowledge that his actions had anything to do with the conflict between his mother and me.

In the end, Boger did me a favor with his testimony. He accused me of living a lie, and of not letting anybody know that I had performed the wedding. So when we had a sidebar discussion after his testimony, I protested that part of Boger's testimony. I felt that I should be allowed to respond to that accusation because, as all of the sidebar participants knew (because they had seen the evidence), I *had* informed my superiors about the wedding, both before the wedding and after it. I hadn't lied about it as Boger claimed.

So Bishop Gwinn agreed that because Boger had brought it in first, I would be allowed to say as part of my testimony that I did inform my superiors of my participation in Tim's wedding. But I wasn't allowed to say there was physical evidence.

When the question came from the jurors, "Is there evidence? Is there physical evidence of what he just said? Is there a written statement?" the answer Bishop Gwinn gave was something like,

"These questions are inappropriate at this stage of the trial." In other words, the evidence was not appropriate to consider in determining whether I was guilty. But, interestingly, once I was found guilty, he ruled that it was appropriate to introduce the physical evidence in the penalty phase of the trial.

This, as well as other rulings, could be appealed, including the seating of the two jurors who said at the outset that they were biased. My counsels said from the start, even throughout the pretrial determinations, there were a number of rulings that could have been appealed. But in the end, I decided not to do that. My counsels urged me to consider appealing; they said it could set a good precedent for future trials. I asked them, "If I won this appeal, would it lead to a retrial?"

They said, "Yes."

I said, "I cannot go through another trial. I just can't. This was all just so emotionally taxing on me and on my family. I don't want another trial."

So, ultimately, we ended up appealing just the penalty. Because if that appeal is heard, it will reverse the penalty, change it, or uphold it; there's not going to be another trial.

Probably the most disturbing thing that happened on the first day of my trial came in the closing statement by the counsel for the church. Chris Fisher gave his closing statement, said, "Thank you," and started to sit down. Then he suddenly stood back up and said he had one more thing to say. He quoted a part of the book of Jude:

> For certain men whose condemnation was written about long ago have secretly slipped in among you. They are godless men who changed the grace of our God into a license for immortality and deny Jesus Christ, our only Sovereign and Lord.

> And although you already know all this, I want to remind you that the Lord delivered his people out of Egypt but later destroyed those who did not believe.

> And the angels who did not keep their positions of authority but abandoned their own home, those he's kept in darkness, bound with everlasting chains for judgment on the great day.

> In a similar way, Sodom and Gomorrah and the surrounding towns gave themselves up to sexual immorality and perversion.

They serve as an example of those who suffer the punishment of eternal fire.

In the very same way, these dreamers pollute their own bodies, rejecting authority, and slander their celestial beings.

But even the archangel Michael, when he was disputing with the devil about the body of Moses, did not dare to bring in a slanderous accusation against him but said the Lord rebuke you.
[Jude 1:4–9]

Then he basically said to the jury that they shouldn't turn the grace of God into a license for immorality and that they would have to give an account for their decision before God.

It was perceived by many as a horrible hate speech.

There were a lot of LGBT supporters in the room, I could tell by the number of rainbow stoles. There were audible gasps while Mr. Fisher was speaking his words of discrimination. I heard the gasp and I looked around, and people were standing. They had risen in silent protest of what they were hearing.

Mr. Fisher stopped speaking and looked to the bishop. "I'm waiting for this disruption to end."

And the bishop said, "You can go ahead and finish, if you will."

So Fisher finished his closing statement.

The first day of the trial was a *long* day. The jury selection took until the lunch recess. And then, although there were only two witnesses, Jon Boger and me, it still took us into the evening hours to conclude the process for day one.

GUILTY

AT DINNER THAT NIGHT, I was hopeful. It seemed like everything had gone well for me. We thought we'd never have a chance to get in any word about my defense. But I did, I got a lot in. I even argued with the scripture, using the parable of the good Samaritan. I said I couldn't refuse my son. I couldn't pass on the other side of the road as the Levite and the priest had done. I had to help my son, who was in need. He was hurting because of what the church had done to him, and I had to help him. I had to perform this marriage. I got all that in and felt good about it.

Bob Coombe had given great opening and closing statements. In fact, people e-mailed me later and asked, "Could I have that speech?" It was that moving and inspirational.

Compared with Boger's testimony and the speech by Fisher, I thought we had done well. I thought I had a chance to be acquitted on both counts. Surely they couldn't side with the counsel for the church, could they? What would *that* mean?

I'm a very optimistic person. I remember asking my counsels at the dinner table that night, "How big would it be if I got acquitted? How big would that be for the LGTB movement in The United Methodist Church?"

They both said, "It would be huge. But it's not going to happen."

But I was still hopeful to the very last second. I expected the verdict to come back not guilty—at least on the second count, and maybe even on both counts.

The jury deliberated during our dinner break. While we were still at dinner, we got notice there would be a verdict that night. I remember feeling nervous as soon as I heard that. I thought, "They're done deliberating already? This can't be good." So we went back into the courtroom after dinner and the jury walked in and sat down. I knew bad news was coming when I saw the jurors were all looking away, avoiding eye contact. Their foreman brought a piece of paper with the verdict to the judge, and he read it.

Guilty on both counts.

The vote on the first charge, that I had performed the wedding, was unanimous. But the decision on the second charge was split. It was not a unanimous vote. Still, the jury had found me guilty on both charges.

It was devastating. In my mind I had tried to prepare myself ahead of time, thinking, "Well, I can't even argue my case, so I'm going to be found guilty." But there was always the hope that, at least on the second charge, I wouldn't be found guilty. And it's one thing to prepare yourself for a guilty verdict, it's another to actually hear it read out loud. I was listening to my church, as a whole, speak against me. You can't prepare for that emotionally. I had tried to prepare myself. But to hear those words uttered in the presence of the whole world—I felt embarrassed and emotionally devastated.

The saddest part of it was that it came from the church I had served for twenty years, the church that had become my spiritual home, a large part of my faith. I chose this church because of the many things I loved about it. All of my children were baptized in The United Methodist Church. To hear my church say those words to me, it was—there is no other word for it—*devastating*.

After the verdict was read, the jurors were dismissed for the night and the court was adjourned until the next morning, for the penalty phase. Bishop Gwinn asked the counsels for the church, as well as my counsels, to stay for another sidebar, during which we negotiated how many witnesses would testify on the second day. Basically, the goal was to eliminate as many as possible. There were just too many to fit into a day's worth of a trial. The counsel for the church had seventeen witnesses; we had twelve. We all agreed if all of them testified we were going to be there for three more days. In the end, we narrowed the witness list down to two church members against and two church members for me, plus Jim Todd, my son Tim, Jon Boger, and me.

Then we discussed the expert witnesses. Unfortunately, we had to eliminate Dr. Paul Fulmer, who had done such excellent research to bolster our case. But we were allowed to have Dr. Thomas Frank and Rev. Janet Wolf as expert witnesses.

Bill Ewing called Thomas Frank on the phone after the sidebar and asked him if he could fly in from North Carolina the next day. Although he was dealing with a family crisis, Dr. Frank agreed to come and give his powerful testimony.

Janet Wolf had been at the trial from the beginning. She wanted to be there for the whole thing, regardless of whether she was going to be called to the stand or not. I felt privileged and honored that all of these wonderful people would take the stand on my behalf. I felt badly about those who had been eliminated as witnesses; they had traveled all that way and stayed the entire first day. Many of them even stayed the second day, even though they were not given the chance to speak.

We stayed at the cabin again that night. My wife, my son, and my daughter went home for the night. I knew my family was devastated by the verdict. I remember seeing a picture a photojournalist took of my daughter, Debbie, hugging me shortly after the guilty verdict was announced. The pain and the disappointment were evident on Debbie's face.

My family commuted back and forth to Camp Innabah. And that was a good thing, really, because my counsels and I had to work hard. We stayed up until one or two o'clock in the morning to prepare for the next day. Poor Bob, my clergy counsel, stayed up even longer. He was still typing when I went to bed, and when I got up the next morning, he was already hard at work again. I wondered if he had gotten any sleep at all that night. There was so much work to do, as we weren't really able to prepare for the second day ahead of time. First, we didn't know whether there was going to be a second day; second, we needed to incorporate the experience of the first day into our statements and defense strategy.

When I finally made it up to my room that night, I checked my e-mails and found a host of requests from the news media—none of which I was able to answer at that time. There were so many e-mails from my friends and family members, and these were so meaningful to me. There was even an e-mail from Jimmy Creech, who had become a good friend and mentor during the pretrial period. His e-mail was short; in fact, it consisted of one sentence: "Dear

Frank, I know how you feel. Love, Jimmy." As I read it, I felt a tear roll down my cheek. I realized that I wasn't alone in this struggle for justice and equality, and that meant the world.

It had been a long and exhausting day. I suspected the next day would be even harder.

THE TRIAL, DAY TWO

THE NEXT MORNING WE were back in the courtroom for the penalty phase of the trial. We got right to the testimony of the witnesses. The first part of the day was devoted to the church witnesses, the second part to the expert witnesses.

Listening to the church witnesses was quite painful; it laid bare the deep split within Zion of Iona, and it brought back terrible memories of the conflicts we had come through. I'm sure others from the church experienced this, as well. I was honored to have Dr. John Schlegel, chairperson of the Staff Parish Relations Committee at Zion Iona, speak on my behalf. If anybody knew what was going on behind the scenes at the church, it was him, and there he was, standing up for me and the ministry I had brought to the church. Then there was Drew Gingrich, a young member of the SPRC committee who made me blush with his accolades about me. I was especially touched when he said: "Frank is the most humble minister I've ever encountered... His Christ-like nature, all these traits to me describe what Christ was."

I remember thinking, "According to some, I'm a rogue. To others, I'm a hero. Go figure."

I was finally allowed to submit into evidence the forms from my profile that showed that I had indeed informed my bishop and my district superintendent about Tim's wedding and my involvement in it.

Jim Todd, my district superintendent, was called by the counsel for the church to testify about a mediation he had overseen in my church, to gauge the situation and people's response to conflict that ensued. He had written a report about it, and that was also allowed into evidence. I thought his testimony was helpful to our side, because it showed that a lot of the conflict in the church had nothing to do with the trial or Tim's wedding.

Then my counsel asked Jim about the statement I made to the bishop in my clergy profile. He didn't deny he had received it, but he said he had never read it.

He said, "Well, it was part of the profile for ministry that everybody has to fill out every year. Every pastor has to fill that out. And we weren't reappointing Frank that year, so I didn't even bother reading through his profile form that year, and I didn't send it to the bishop for the same reason."

I was surprised and dismayed. But, regardless, I appreciated his testimony on the state of Zion of Iona. The witnesses against me were saying, "Frank's act of violating the *Discipline* destroyed the church. This wedding he performed, when it came out, it destroyed the whole church. Financially the church was ruined and it had *all* to do with that wedding."

Jim's testimony helped corroborate my witnesses who said the conflict had little to do with the wedding. It was an internal struggle that had been going on for a long time.

And then my son, Tim, was called to testify. That was very emotional for him, for me, for my family, and I think for a lot of people in the courtroom. When he took the stand and started sharing his story, I had a hard time. I couldn't hide my tears. In fact, I was sobbing. And I heard sobbing going on behind me. I knew my family was crying. I didn't actually look back. I couldn't.

Tim shared how he grew up as a preacher's kid, and how his faith was so important to him. He told how he had gone with me to that annual conference when he was thirteen years old and already knew that he was homosexual. He talked about realizing that his church was saying that he was not normal, that he was a freak of nature, that he was sinful and somehow outside of the grace of God. He talked about how that had plunged him into a depression that ended up so bad he considered suicide. He had suicidal thoughts. He had even come up with a plan for committing suicide.

It was an emotional moment, and not just for me. One of our supporters, Richard Kirk, had a very similar story. He later told me he was in tears hearing Tim's story. And he shared with me, "I just lost it emotionally, because here I was hearing the story of a man who is thirty years younger than I am, and he's telling the exact same story of what happened to me. So things have not really changed that much in thirty years."

Then my son was questioned, cross-examined, and he did well. I was so proud of him. But then the counsel for the church asked an interesting question.

Chris Fisher said, "We saw in the news this weekend—maybe you didn't want this to be known, but now everybody knows it—that you are no longer married. Could you see yourself asking your father to perform another wedding for you in the future?"

My son said, "That's not accurate, actually. I am married."

He was in the process of getting a divorce. His relationship with Bobby had not worked out. But the divorce wasn't final until later in December, so he was still married at that point.

My counsel raised an objection to the question, and there was another sidebar.

The judge asked if Tim was divorced. I said, "No, he's not divorced. At this point he's not divorced."

Then the judge asked Chris Fisher, "Do you have evidence for the divorce?"

Fisher said, "No, not here, but it's on the grounds."

I didn't know it at the time, but they did have some document. I saw it later on. Actually, Jon Boger sent it to me after the trial was over. But that document clearly said that the divorce was not final until December 27. Apparently, Massachusetts has a long waiting period before a divorce becomes final; probably to give the couple ample time for reconciliation.

As we continued to debate, Chris Fisher said, "Well, okay, maybe we don't want to get into that."

But he had already made it public, so he got it in.

I said something like, "Look, I'm going to testify. You can ask me if I intend to do other weddings. You don't have to ask my son."

Finally, the whole line of questioning was disallowed by Bishop Gwinn.

It was hard for Tim to testify. He said it was very emotional, although I couldn't really tell it at the time. He handled himself so well. The turmoil was internal.

The day continued with plenty of drama. There was a showdown between Bishop Gwinn and the LGBT supporters in the audience. Rev. Wolf gave her testimony, which was quite power-ful. She talked about restorative justice, as opposed to retributive justice. She said you don't want to have to go to an extreme, because justice in the Bible as well as in the *Discipline* is not really about punishment; it's about restoring a person back into the community. Her presentation was so good, and what she said was so insightful that people in the courtroom began to applaud.

That was the only time I saw Bishop Gwinn rattled. He had to stop it, of course. After he'd allowed the people to stand in si-lent protest the day before, Fisher had reminded him that he had ruled that no demonstrations of any kind would be allowed in the courtroom.

Bishop Gwinn was very charming. His Southern accent under-lined his warm, hospitable personality. I was actually quite taken by his way of addressing us and the public. When people started applauding Rev. Wolf, he was visibly agitated. Still, his words were so kind. He raised his voice a bit and said, "If something like that should ever happen again, we will invite you to leave the room."

I thought, "Wow. We're not going to kick you out. We're going to invite you to leave." I was so impressed with him.

I was supposed to take the witness stand one last time after the lunch recess. My defense team and I wanted to explain to the court how I had evolved from a silent LGBT supporter to an outspoken advocate and activist. As part of my advocacy role, I had called "discriminatory" the language in the *Discipline* that deals with homosexuality. I had publicly called on The United Methodist Church to end its discrimination against the LGBT community. I had pointed out that the exclusionary policies of the church were causing harm to our gay and lesbian brothers and sisters, as it had done harm to my son.

My defense team felt it was crucial to explain my concerns about exclusionary policies, as on the previous day my defense was based on the argument, "I may have violated a rule of the *Discipline*, but I did it as an act of love for my son, who had been harmed by the church's doctrine." My argument had been along the philosophical lines of: an act of compassion takes precedence over a religious law. To this end I had invoked the parable of the good Samaritan.

My counsels worked with me on a very carefully crafted state-ment, and I received quite a bit of coaching. "Don't say this, but do say that. Don't use that word, say it this way..."

We knew already that Fisher would ask me during cross-examination, "Will you promise never to do a gay wedding again?"

I was supposed to answer, "I cannot answer this question," and then elaborate by saying that I didn't know whether I would or would not agree to perform another gay wedding because it was a hypothetical question. Nobody can exactly predict their actions of the future.

As I said, my defense for Day Two was carefully crafted. The hope was that I would receive a mild penalty. We were hoping for a reprimand at that point.

And at first I felt all right with this approach. I didn't want to lose my job, my career, my calling, after all. But as the time approached for me to take the stand again, I knew I had to tell the court where my heart was. I had to tell them that the church, our United Methodist Church, was harming people every day, and it had to stop. I knew I had to take a stand for my gay children, for my family, and for all LGBT members of the church. The thought of tiptoeing around the issue and giving in to the church's pressure made me feel angry at myself. I had to tell the truth. I knew I had to take a stand, no matter what would happen next. And, deep down, I also knew that testifying to all that would surely lead to my defrocking.

So when we broke for lunch that day, I prayed. I prayed hard. It was an intense and desperate prayer. I remember being physically tired. I'd hardly gotten any sleep the night before, and I was just exhausted emotionally. And, honestly, I wasn't sure whether I could do it. I wasn't sure I was strong enough. I felt like I had to muster all of my strength to stand up against this big church, in front of the whole world, and say what I felt in my heart. I wasn't sure whether the words were going to come out of my mouth or not.

That's when I went down on my knees in the privacy of my room in the cabin. I had a talk with God. I prayed out loud, and I didn't care if people could hear me on the other side of the door. I needed God to hear me.

I said, "God, I don't know what to do. I need some assurance. If I tell the court how I really feel, what does that mean for me? It could mean that I'm going to be defrocked. Is that what I have to do? Is that what you want me to do?"

As I prayed, I wondered what it would mean for my family, as well. I thought about my two sons who were still in school, who needed my financial support. I thought about my paycheck and our health insurance. How would I live? What else would I do if I was defrocked? Ministry is the only thing I had done for the past twenty years. What would I do for work? What would Brigitte and I live on? I threw all those questions at God because I was scared.

And suddenly I had a thought; it was like God was reminding me of what Jesus went through. Maybe that's a thought that comes naturally to Christians, but I really thought about it in a new light. I thought about what Jesus gave up. He gave up his entire life. He was falsely accused and even tortured, and he gave up his life willingly in the name of love, to show a better way—he took the high road. What Jesus did was the ultimate act of love for humanity. And I thought, "Okay, considering what Jesus did, what he gave up, losing my paycheck and my health insurance doesn't seem like such a scary thing anymore."

Of course, it still felt huge. But compared to what Christ and other martyrs had done, it wasn't that big of a deal. I specifically thought of Jan Hus, who was a forerunner of Martin Luther. Hus was burned at the stake for taking a stand. I thought, "Now, *that's* a sacrifice. You can't even compare losing your job to giving up your life."

From that moment on, I knew what I had to do. And I knew I had to talk to my counsels about it, because they had been working so hard on my statement. They had worked so hard on my behalf, and now I was effectively throwing out all that hard work. Telling my counsels was the first hurdle before I took the stand.

A lot of my supporters from the church were at the trial, and several of them were hanging out in our cabin during the court recesses. So it turned out that I told my pastoral assistant, Clydette, about my decision first. She was the first person I ran into when I came out of my room. I shared with her what I felt I had to say to the court.

She replied, with great concern in her voice, "You know that means they're going to defrock you, don't you?"

I said, "I know. But I have to be honest. I'm going to have to tell them where I stand on this. I just have to."

She said again, "You know that means you're going to be defrocked?"

And I said, "I know."

Then I told my counsels. I actually waited until we were sitting at the table in the courtroom to do so. I didn't tell them at the cabin. I didn't have the guts then. I had to muster my courage. To my surprise, they both said, "Frank, you've got to go with your heart. Whatever the Holy Spirit tells you, you've got to go with your heart. Do it. We're okay with it. We stand by you. We support you."

That was a huge relief.

But as the time came for me to take the stand, I got physically sick. I had scribbled down some words, what I was going to say, and it was messy. Moreover, my thoughts were all jumbled. I was so nervous, I felt sick to my stomach. And when you're sick to your stomach, you feel weak. I didn't know whether I could actually say the words. It was that dramatic for me, that traumatic to stand before the church and tell the truth, to stand up for what I believed and for what is right.

When I sat down in the stand, I looked over to my family. Behind them, I saw a sea of people wearing rainbow-colored stoles. And it dawned on me that I had more support in this room than I had opposition. I looked around and saw people smiling at me, nodding and encouraging me. It was almost like I felt their strength, their support, and their prayers. And suddenly, I knew I could do it. I felt strength returning to my stomach. I could feel my confidence coming back, the confidence I needed to take a stand. I knew then that I *would* take a stand. And the words would come out right. It was an amazing feeling, really, just amazing. It was like going from fear to courage, carried along by the prayers of my family and my supporters.

I started by telling the court about my ministry at Zion of Iona, how the church was becoming a diverse and accepting place of ministry. I shared about my deep-seated commitment to equality, my desire to minister to every person. I said I had never refused ministry to anybody, no matter what.

Then I explained how I found myself in new territory, after it became known that I had performed my gay son's wedding ceremony. People asked me questions, the press asked me about my theology, and I was transformed into a public advocate for our LGBT brothers and sisters. I said that I could no longer go back to being a silent supporter; I was going to continue to be an advocate. That was my new calling from God.

Then came the part I had been so afraid of…and the words just flowed, they came out exactly right. In fact, one of the first things I looked up in the official court transcript was this statement. I wanted to see, thinking, "Am I really remembering this right? Did these words all come out so well?" I read through it and said, "Wow, yes. It really did."

And I realized that was not just me talking. I truly was empowered by the Holy Spirit. I thought of the passage in Mark 13:11:

> Whenever you are arrested and brought to trial, do not worry beforehand about what to say. Just say whatever is given you at the time, for it is not you speaking, but the Holy Spirit.

According to the official court transcript, this is exactly what I said to the court:

> So before you make a decision, please know that I will continue to minister to all people equally, regardless of their gender, nationality, race, social status, economic status, or sexual orientation. And my message is going to be that we as a church and as individuals need to stop judging people based on their sexual orientation or anything else. We have to stop the hate speech. We have to stop treating them as second-class Christians. We have to stop harming beloved children of God. We have to reach out to them and treat them as Jesus would have treated them. That's going to be my message. [*You can read the entire testimony in the Appendix of this book.*]

At that point I reached into my pocket and pulled out a rainbow-colored stole. Bill Ewing, my attorney, had given it to me earlier that day. He said, "My wife wants you to have this. This is from my wife."

I took the stole out of my jacket pocket and said, "I don't think things happen by chance. I was given a stole and it is a rainbow stole. And if I am permitted, Bishop, to wear it, I would like to put this on as a sign that I will make a covenant from this day forth never to be silent again. Is it okay, Bishop, to put that on me?"

Bishop Gwinn allowed it. I put on the stole and continued, looking straight at the jurors:

"I will wear this as a visible symbol for you to understand that this is what I have to do from now on. That's all I have to say."

The testimony I had given on the previous day left me feeling nervous. I wasn't sure it was good enough to get me acquitted. But after my uncompromising testimony on the second day, when I finally stood up for my beliefs and for all those whom the church has harmed and discriminated against, I remember feeling very calm. I was at peace with myself, with God, and with the world. I didn't care anymore what the church could or would do to me.

But I was not done in the stand. The counsel for the church, Chris Fisher, rose to proceed with the cross-examination. He seemed pleased with my testimony. I could see it in his demeanor. He asked, "Are you willing to repent of your actions you have been found guilty of and renounce your disobedience to the *Discipline* of The United Methodist Church?"

I answered, "I cannot."

He asked a second question: "Will you promise from henceforth never to perform another same-sex wedding and ceremony and from henceforth to uphold all the provisions of the *Discipline*?"

I answered, "I cannot make that statement."

He had no further questions. That's all he needed.

I was dismissed from the stand.

GO DEFROCK YOURSELF

AFTER THE JURY HAD BEEN dismissed for deliberations on my penalty, I had two statements prepared for the press, because there was going to be a press conference immediately after the trial.

The first statement was the one I would give if I was defrocked. It started out, "This just goes to show that the church has chosen law over love. There's so much work to do. And the discrimination has to stop." It went on from there.

The second statement, in case I was not defrocked, started out, "Today we saw a victory. Grace triumphed over law."

It was all right there on two index cards.

But the penalty the court delivered was somewhere in between. It was complicated, and neither of my statements really fit.

The trial court said that I was suspended from all duties for thirty days. And within those thirty days I had to come up with an answer to this question: Given your new ministry and your new calling to be an advocate for the LGTB community, can you still uphold the *Discipline* in its entirety?

In other words, "You have thirty days to denounce gay marriage."

It really was an interesting penalty. In some sense I think it was genius, and in another way cowardly, because they basically told me to defrock myself.

In effect, they were saying, "We don't want to defrock you. We know the whole world is watching, so we don't want to do it. We leave you to go ahead and do it yourself."

Immediately after the jury was dismissed from the courtroom, a series of loud noises erupted behind me. Matt and several others at Reconciling Ministries Network had thought of a way to "make a statement" at the end of the trial in case I got defrocked: LGBT supporters were supposed to turn over their chairs in a symbolic reenactment of Jesus turning over the tables in a temple that had been corrupted by the politics of priests and ruthless merchants. Even though I knew of this action ahead of time, the tossing of the chairs startled me. I was also confused over what this meant in light of the penalty; did the RMN folks think my penalty equaled a defrocking? Then people broke out singing the spiritual, "Were You There When They Crucified My Lord?"

The next thing I knew, Matt Berryman had found me and guided me to a makeshift communion table. Steve Heiss, a pastor who was also under complaint for performing same-sex weddings in his church, was praying over a loaf of bread. The last time I had seen Steve was in a setting of a different communion. We had met at a coffee shop in Wilkes Barre, Pennsylvania, as United Methodist pastors who were both facing a complaint for performing same-sex marriages. It was the beginning of a friendship.

Matt asked me if I could pray over the communion cup. It was all like a dream to me. But my pastoral instincts took over, and I lifted the cup and started reciting a part of the Great Thanksgiving. I didn't think anything of the cameras that were all around me. Then Steve and I gave communion to about eighty supporters who remained, and that was a meaningful moment. I felt like I was spiritually connecting with people who had become my friends through the experience of the trial.

So, when I left the court that day, I had not been defrocked. I had been given a thirty-day suspension, at the end of which I had to appear before the Board of Ordained Ministry of my conference and say, "Yes, I will uphold the letter of the law," or, "No, I will not."

Immediately, a reporter asked me at the post-trial press conference, "Will you do another wedding? If somebody asked you right now to do another same-sex wedding, would you do it?"

I said, "Yeah, absolutely."

"So does this mean that you're going to be defrocked after the thirty days?"

I said, "Well, probably."

Immediately after the trial, I went on a "press tour." I was fortunate to have Cathy Husid-Shamir of Husid National Media to handle press requests and coordinate my schedule. I felt that responding to requests for interviews was an important aspect of my LGBT advocacy, especially in a church whose leadership had to date denied the fact that its constituency was divided over the issue of LTBG inclusion and marriage rights. In fact, the very next day I had an opportunity to speak on Tamron Hall's *NewsNation*. I also talked with Jake Tapper of CNN, Aljazeera's *America Today*, NPR radio, a few regional TV channels, and a lot of local news channels. I did many phone interviews with newspapers, as well. It was like a whirlwind, but Cathy spaced it out perfectly; she had a whole itinerary for me and coached me for every appointment.

Although it was important for me to talk to the media, it also caused some stress, coming on the heels of the emotionally taxing trial. After the initial burst of media interest things calmed down, and I finally had time to process what had happened and what my next steps would be. I pondered what the penalty meant for me. What was I going to do with this? Did I just hand in my credentials? That's what I felt the jury was asking of me. If I couldn't swear to uphold a law I knew was wrong, I was supposed to just hand in my credentials. This request seemed mean-spirited to me.

I thought, "No, I'm not going to do that." That was clear to me almost from the beginning. I wasn't going to voluntarily surrender my credentials, because I felt that would amount to deserting the LGTB community in the church. I had promised to be an advocate. So that part of the jury's request had already been answered in my mind.

But then I wasn't sure how to answer the first part of the penalty, the part that asked if I could uphold the *Discipline*. In my mind, I was upholding the *Discipline* by refusing to discriminate against my LGBT brothers and sisters. So again I talked with my counselors and with so many pastors and even a few bishops who called me during that time. Each of them said, "Don't hand in your credentials."

They all gave slightly different rationales, but what I heard people say could be summarized like this: "You can say that you can uphold the entire *Discipline*. You can say it and basically have your own interpretation of it, because the truth is that nobody can really uphold the entire *Discipline*. Nobody can uphold the entire *Discipline*, because the *Discipline* contradicts itself."

I believe that refusing to perform a same-sex marriage ceremony is actually against the *Discipline*. So people were saying to me, "Just tell them, 'I can uphold the *Discipline* in its entirety just like everybody else does.'"

In the meantime, I was having talks with my district superintendent, because I was supposed to have supervisory meetings with him, according to the penalty. During one of those supervisory meetings, Bishop Johnson joined us. My wife and I met with Jim Todd and the bishop at Grandview United Methodist Church in Lancaster County.

I could tell that Bishop Johnson had taken the trial to heart; she didn't seem like herself. During an NPR radio interview in which she, Tim, and I appeared as guests, she said that she had received some 400 pieces of hate mail during the time of the trial and in the aftermath. I assumed she read them all and they affected her emotionally. Apparently, she was devastated. I sensed that she felt bad for what we had been put through under her watch.

After many talks with a variety of people, after much deliberation and prayer, I came to the following conclusion about the penalty: I could not say that I could uphold the entire *Discipline* and then have my own interpretation of it. If I were to say, "Yes, I can uphold it," I would have to be honest and give an explanation of what my interpretation of the statement was.

Jim Todd had made it clear to me that, "Yes, I can uphold the *Discipline* in its entirety," was the *only* answer the Board of Ordained Ministry would take as a "Yes." If I were to make that statement but added *anything* after that, if I qualified the "Yes" in any way, it would be counted as a "No."

And that I couldn't do. I could not just say, "Yes, I can uphold the *Discipline* in its entirety," without any qualifying statement or interpretation. It was a matter of conscience. I knew I couldn't do it.

And still people tried to convince me, "Yes, you can do it. You can have your own interpretation and you can say it. That's basically what every single clergy person in The United Methodist Church is doing. That's why we're still The 'United' Methodist Church, because everybody is basically doing that."

But it did not feel right to me. Making a statement like that without qualification, I would not have been true to myself or to my conscience.

So I decided I needed to hold a press conference and make a statement *before* I went to be interviewed by the Board of Ordained Ministry. According to the court, I had to make my statement in front of the Board of Ordained Ministry in written form as well as verbally.

So I thought, "You know what? I'm going to actually have to make a statement before I make my statement to the board, because if I don't, it looks like I'm handing in my credentials. And I am not going to do that."

I felt that I needed to schedule a press conference ahead of my meeting with the Board. I decided to hold it at Arch Street United Methodist Church in Philadelphia, because it was an official reconciling church, because of Pastor Hynicka's support, and because the church had hosted the historic mass-clergy same-sex marriage ceremony a few weeks before my trial.

Pastor Hynicka opened the press conference with a devotion and opening remarks. I then gave my statement and entertained questions. I proclaimed, "First of all, my statement is that I *cannot* uphold the *Discipline* because it contains discriminatory laws. Secondly, I will *not* voluntarily hand in my credentials. I perceive a calling to be a voice for the LGBT community within The United Methodist Church, and turning in my credentials would be like betraying my calling and the LGBT community. If they want my credentials, they will have to take them from me, because I will not give them up voluntarily."

The second part of the press conference was about presenting a petition to Bishop Johnson. By this time the outcome of my trial had already caused an uproar among the progressives in The United Methodist Church and beyond, so much so that petitions were signed and presented to church leaders demanding in no uncertain terms: "Stop the trials." The Reconciling United Methodist group and I put together a petition for Bishop Johnson and decided to present it to her with a number of the pastors who had performed the mass-clergy ceremony. I felt that lending my support for the petition was the least I could to for my colleagues who had stood up for me. We were calling for a moratorium on all LGBT-related trials in the church.

Bishop Johnson responded to the petition almost immediately. She acknowledged the call for a moratorium and promised to do all in her power to prevent any future trials going forth. In addition, she called the homophobic, exclusionary laws in the *Discipline* "discriminatory." As a result, none of the clergy members who performed the wedding has been charged to this date.

The Thursday after the press conference, on December 19, I had to appear before the Board of Ordained Ministry. The board members already knew what to expect, because of my statement to the press. As I entered the room with the thirty-five to forty board members, I had a sense that everything seemed to be predetermined. I had expected some deliberations or a vote, but no, it was all prearranged. I walked in, and maybe 15 minutes later it was done.

After Mindy Connelly, the chairperson of the board, opened the meeting with a prayer, I was asked for my statement. I read the statement out loud, and turned the written statement over to her. It was the same statement I had given at my press conference just three days before saying, "No, I cannot uphold the *Discipline* as a whole because it contains laws and language that are homophobic and discriminatory. And no, I will not surrender my credentials voluntarily."

Mindy said, "So, that's it then. Based on your statement, your credentials are surrendered."

I replied, "Well, I made it pretty clear that I will not surrender my credentials voluntarily."

She nodded and said, "Yes, I know. We are taking them from you."

Mindy then asked those who were comfortable to come to the front, where I sat, and place a hand on my head or shoulders to say a prayer for me. I experienced this as a moment of reaching out and rejection all at the same time. It later occurred to me that this is exactly the experience of our LGBT sisters and brothers in The United Methodist Church: "We welcome you in, but we reject your lifestyle and deny your marriage rights and your calling to be pastoral leaders."

I felt for some of the members on the board, actually. They were mostly clergy, with a few lay members. Mindy, the chairperson, was actually one of my supporters. She's a wonderful person with a heart as big as you will find for the LGBT community. She had tears in her eyes when I greeted her coming in, and she said, "You know that what we must do here today is not what I want to do, right?"

Other pastors came to me after the meeting, and they were visibly upset. I remember one of them saying, "This is not right. This is horrible. I disagree with this. I am ashamed to be a part of this."

But there were others on the board who agreed that what was happening to me was right and just. One of my colleagues, whom I had known from a joint ministry we did together some fifteen years ago, said to me, "When this is all over, I want to sit down and talk to you sometime." He was convinced that I had gone awry in my theology on human sexuality.

I don't think the board members had any choice in the matter. My counsels had, by accident, gotten hold of some e-mail exchanges between Bishop Johnson, Superintendent Todd, and Bill Waddell, the highest attorney of The United Methodist Church. (He is sometimes referred to as the chancellor.) He had also served as Bishop Gwinn's attorney during my trial, and he regularly works as an attorney for the Council of Bishops. These communications clearly showed that the Board of Ordained Ministry was carefully instructed about how to proceed in my interview with them; that's why Jim Todd knew about it ahead of time and had communicated "the rules" to me. That's why the Board of Ordained Ministry never took a vote.

In fact, a statement for the press had already been prepared. The conference communications director had it all printed up and ready to go as soon as I came out of the conference room. The church's press statement itself confirmed my original suspicion that they were going to put this all on me. The statement claimed that because of my refusal to uphold the *Discipline* in its entirety, my credentials were now deemed surrendered by the church. In other words, they implied that I had defrocked myself. The church can deem all it wants, but the truth is that they took my credentials. I did not surrender them!

When my wife and I left the conference center and got into our car, she said, "Look at your hands."

I looked down and saw that my hands were shaking. Even before I was able to get in touch with my feelings at that point, I was visibly shaken by the experience. And it was no wonder. I had just been rejected and politically ousted by the church I had served for twenty years because I refused to discriminate against God's beloved children. But at the center of it all stood an act of love I performed for my son.

And what was my actual crime? What had I done? I blessed the love and commitment of two people who were in love with each other; they just happened to be of the same gender. Doesn't the Church realize that there is no such thing as a victimless crime? There were no victims in this act of love I performed. If anything, it strengthened the commitment of two lovers and it strengthened the bonds of love between a father and son.

So, as of that day, I was unemployed. My contract with the Zion of Iona United Methodist Church was "deemed" terminated. I was no longer an employee. We were lucky that we didn't live in a parsonage. We had owned our home for many years, or else we would have found ourselves having to deal with moving out right at Christmas.

THE AFTERMATH

AS MINISTERS, WE HOLD our membership in The United Methodist Church through our membership as clergy in the conference. We don't have a membership in any local church. So when the church defrocked me, it also ended my membership in the church. I had been *de facto* "excommunicated." I found myself without a faith community for the first time in my life.

On December 22, just three days after I was defrocked, Brigitte and I joined the Foundry United Methodist Church in Washington, D.C., along with our sons Kevin and Pascal. On first blush, this might not seem to make sense. Why would anybody rejoin an organization that had just kicked him out?

However, it was important to me to rejoin The United Methodist Church because I had made a commitment, especially to the LGTB community within the church, and I wanted them to know, "I'm not leaving. I will continue to speak from within the church."

A day after I was defrocked, Rev. Dean Snyder, the pastor at Foundry, who was a great supporter and friend throughout my trial, contacted me and invited me to come to D.C. the next Sunday. He said, "Why don't you plan on preaching, Frank? I think we need to hear a word from you. And I think you need to be among United Methodist *friends*."

I was touched by his offer and accepted. Foundry United Methodist Church has been a beacon of hope in our denomination for many years, and it is well known for its LGBT advocacy. I remember thinking, "I would not mind being a member of Foundry."

A couple of days later I called Dean back and said, "What do you think about our family joining Foundry this Sunday?"

He said, "I love it!"

I'm really glad we did this. Foundry actually live-streamed the entire service. And it was widely covered by the United Methodist news agencies in addition to some Washington media outlets. So I had the honor of speaking that Sunday, and my message to all United Methodists was, "If you're thinking about leaving the Methodist Church, don't. Because we need you. We need you in our fight. We need you to help us change the *Discipline*, to get rid of the discriminatory and exclusionary laws."

I continued, "I sincerely believe that we as United Methodists have been taken captive. We have been living in homophobic captivity since 1972, the year homophobic language was first introduced into the *Book of Discipline*. This is not us. We're not homophobic people. We have always been proud of being a diverse people. We are an inclusive, not an exclusive, people."

I continued sharing about how the church's founder, John Wesley, had sought to include everybody in the then fledgling Methodist movement, how he went to the street corners and even into the prison system.

And let's not forget Wesley's three simple rules for living: "Do no harm, do good, and stay in love with God."

That's who we are as United Methodists—God-loving people who do good, not people who do harm.

Foundry supported us in so many ways, even financially. The congregation took a love offering for us and made an appeal on the Internet for other churches and individuals to join in this effort. So when I returned to Foundry for a special service together with Jimmy Creech and Beth Stroud on January 31, 2014, they presented us with a check for over $31,000, as a love offering.

That's a message in and of itself. The leadership of The United Methodist Church defrocked me, and the true and faithful part of the church, the inclusive side, sent a message loud and clear: "God is not going to let you down if you stand up for what's right. And we're doing our part in supporting you."

As Dean Snyder stated, "It is a statement to all progressive leaders in The United Methodist Church, which is saying: 'Don't be afraid to take risks for justice. God will not let you down. The church may threaten to take away your paycheck, but don't let that intimidate you; there will be support for you and your family!'"

My conscience compelled me take a stand—to risk my career, my income, and my security without any guarantees, and I lost it all. But that's not where the story ended. It's been amazing to see how God has provided me and my family with everything we needed, even through The United Methodist Church.

Another amazing development was that I never actually found myself out of work. On paper, I may have been unemployed as of December 19, 2013. But since that day, I have received invitations to speak or preach in many different venues. I have spoken at engagements all over the country. I'm preaching almost every Sunday, mostly in United Methodist churches. And I frequently receive honorariums, so I can continue to provide for my family's needs. I sometimes say, "For a defrocked minister, I am awfully busy."

One thing is sure: What people meant for harm, God has turned into a new and exciting ministry. Everywhere I go, I meet people who thank me for the stand I have taken. Many of them are gays, lesbians, bisexuals, or transgendered. Many of them have tears in their eyes, and they say things like, "I have never heard such words of affirmation for me from a minister or from a church." My family's story, the act of love for my son, my subsequent stance against discrimination, and my message of God's love for all people—no one excluded—is bringing healing and change to the church.

Initially, I was also worried about health insurance. Luckily, our insurance premium was paid through December 31. And, luckily for us, the Affordable Care Act kicked in on January 1. So we're covered under the Act, through a local plan here in Pennsylvania, and it's actually better coverage than we had before.

And another God-thing happened on the very day after I was defrocked. After my meeting with the Board of Ordained Ministry in Philadelphia, my media coordinator, Cathy Husid-Shamir, had lined up two interviews, one with Anderson Cooper and another with Laurence O'Donnell, for which I had to be in an uplink studio in downtown Philadelphia until 9 p.m.

I was interviewed by CNN in the morning. Then I had interviews and appointments in New York City all day long. I had a bit of a break in the middle of the day—the only two-hour window of time I had between interviews—during which I received two phone calls. One was from Rev. Patrick Bruns, pastor of the Boulder United Methodist Church in Colorado, who wanted to thank me for taking a stand and to invite me to come speak at his church. The second phone call was also encouraging—and ended up being so much more. It came from Bishop Minerva Carcaño of the California-Pacific Conference. I had never met her or talked with her before, and I remember being really surprised at her call.

She said, "I'm calling you, my brother, to let you know that you have support here on the West Coast and especially in our conference (the California-Pacific Conference). I want you to know that I have talked to several pastors and district superintendents, and we want you to know that we stand behind you and we think what you did was right. You acted in the spirit of Jesus."

I remember getting teary-eyed as she talked. I couldn't put it into words then, but it was an amazing feeling to be affirmed by a leader of the church after another body of the church had found me guilty of wrongdoing.

What she said next was even more exciting.

"Please don't share this with anybody yet," she said, "but we want to invite you to come and minister in our conference as a United Methodist pastor."

At that point she said she wanted to clear that decision with Bishop Johnson first, and then she was going to make a statement about it. And not long after, that's what she did. I remember saying to her, "Thank you so much, Bishop. You just made my life—not just my day, but my life!"

In a statement posted on the website of the California-Pacific Annual Conference of The United Methodist Church, Bishop Carcaño wrote:

> Brothers and Sisters,
>
> I want you to know that on this day following in the footsteps of Bishop Kennedy and with the support of his bishop, Bishop Peggy Johnson, I invited the Rev. Frank Schaefer to come and join us in ministry in the California-Pacific Conference…
>
> While I recognize that our brother Frank has been defrocked by those in authority in his conference, I believe that those who have acted in such a way have done so in obedience to the *Book of Discipline* of The United Methodist Church, an imperfect book of human law that violates the very spirit of Jesus the Christ who taught

us through word and deed that all God's children are of sacred worth and welcomed into the embrace of God's grace. I believe that the time has come for we United Methodists to stand on the side of Jesus and declare in every good way that The United Methodist Church is wrong in its position on homosexuality, wrong in its exclusion of our LGBTQ brothers and sisters, and wrong in its incessant demand to determine through political processes who can be fully members of the body of Christ. Frank Schaefer chose to stand with Jesus as he extended love and care to his gay son and his partner. We should stand with him and others who show such courage and faithfulness.

One official and powerful organ of the church might have found me guilty and ultimately rejected me, but another part of the church, led by Bishop Carcaño, was welcoming me back.

That was a huge boost for me, to know that I could still be in ministry. And it was a huge statement she was making to the church. It also reveals the tremendous division we are facing in The United Methodist Church.

Bishop Carcaño acknowledged in the statement that she does not have the power to reissue an ordination for me. So I would receive a license and work as a licensed local pastor. But still, for me to be invited to serve as a United Methodist minister in a United Methodist Church, with all rights and duties—a license is no less than an ordination in that sense—that's huge.

Bishop Carcaño, her cabinet, and her conference are taking a stand, a big stand against the discrimination that's going on against the LGBT community within the denomination. And, as expected, she has received criticism for it. On January 10, 2014, I met with Bishop Carcaño in California and committed to the appointment process, which is still under way.

MY FAMILY'S
CONTINUED JOURNEY

THE TRIAL DEFINITELY TOOK a toll on Brigitte and my children. We certainly have a lot to digest and work through with all that transpired, but it seems we can't shake our Methodist roots. There's so much to love and admire about the Methodist Church, and we still believe that the Methodist Church will rid itself of discriminatory and exclusionary policies.

But there is one thing we also gained as a family through this church trial: our family bonds are stronger than ever before. When we were all together to celebrate Christmas right after my defrocking, we celebrated the fact that we are an LGBT family, and that our family's love is strong enough to stand up to any bully, even a powerful organization that may threaten us with grave consequences.

We also learned that we are not alone; through this ordeal, we met so many good people who supported and encouraged us. We have more friends than ever before—really good friends that make sacrifices for us.

And last, but most important, we learned that God rewards those who live out the principle of love, who are willing to take the high road of forgiveness, and who are willing to stand up for justice. In the end our faith was stronger, because God never let us down.

The United Methodist denomination did, but not God. On the contrary, God kept providing for us.

The Schaefer family in 2009.

FIVE POINTS FOR THE CHURCH'S STRUGGLE WITH HOMOSEXUALITY

SEVERAL PEOPLE HAVE ASKED me in Q&A sessions and interviews about the biblical texts that seem to condemn homosexuality. This is what I see the church struggle with the most.

People have used and continue to use a few passages in the Bible to justify discrimination and hateful speech against the LGBT community. But there are reasonable, thoughtful, and compelling arguments to be made against such interpretations. In fact, these arguments have been made by plenty of scholars, pastors, and theologians.

Many of these progressive theologians have considered the context, culture, historic settings, as well as scientific knowledge about homosexuality, and have concluded that these texts are not really talking about what we are talking about today: They are not talking about loving, committed homosexual relationships.

Because the scholarly arguments from the Bible have already been proposed and corroborated many times, I will not duplicate these arguments here, but I would like to include some general, commonsense observations. The conflict we are facing in the Christian church as a whole (United Methodist and otherwise) is rooted in our view of the inspiration of our holy writ, the scriptures, the Bible. There are two basic camps.

The *literalists* claim a verbal inspiration that leads them to read the scriptures as direct, word-by-word instructions by God.

And then you have the *contextualists*, who claim that the scriptures need to be interpreted in their context. Sometimes a passage can be taken at face value, but the way the Bible was written typically demands that we work to interpret a passage within its wider context. Most contextualists believe scripture is inspired by God, but they usually acknowledge that some passages reflect author biases, factual inconsistencies, and misunderstandings.

——I believe a biblical view of sexuality must take these five points about reading and interpreting scripture into account:

1. Since Christ frequently spoke in parables and metaphors, we have been given an example of applying scripture beyond a literal reading. Also, because Christ did not condemn homosexuality, this issue was either not as vital a topic as some conservatives make it out to be or he didn't consider that we would face such confusion about his silence these 2,000 years later.

2. Christ teaches us how to interpret scriptures in Matthew 22:36-40, proclaiming that our lens for interpreting all scripture ("All the Law and the Prophets hang on these two commandments.") should be love for God and love for neighbor. There can be no interpretation of scripture that goes against this, or that separates, condemns, judges, or otherwise discriminates against anyone. If there is any question, given this lens of interpretation, Christians should always come down on the side of love.

3. Some scripture passages require a metaphorical reading, such as Isaiah 11:12, Psalm 22:28, and Revelation 7:1, which talk about the "four corners of the earth," suggesting that the earth is flat. Yet very few believers today would oppose the fact that the earth is spherical. Just as we possess new insights into the nature of the cosmos, new knowledge in our understanding of human sexuality exists today and we must allow for the fact that the ancient understanding was different than our modern understanding of many things, including sexual orientation.

4. A consistent literalist interpretation of scripture is simply not possible in light of several biblical passages that call for irrelevant and abusive actions. For instance, Exodus 21:7-9 details how a father should go about selling his daughter into slavery. I dare say

that nobody today would publicly defend a literalist reading of this passage. Every written communication requires context in order to interpret it correctly. Taking scripture out of context or trying to remove its context entirely will never lead to correct theology. Every scripture is the inspired word of God, but that does not mean the entire Bible is literally and universally applicable.

Without reason and contextualization, we would have to condone slavery and genocide, and accept the ancient biblical view that considered women and children as property. Today, even literalists admit that those views constitute discrimination.

5. The Reformed Church has long embraced the concept of two sources of divine revelation—the book of scripture and the "book of nature." The fact that God created LGBT children shows that we should be accepting of them. The irrefutable evidence today is that, just like gender, sexual orientation is *not* a choice. In a very real sense, then, condemning homosexuals for the way they were created is condemning God's creation. And who wants to be found guilty of doing that?

The church will have to change its interpretation of homosexuality, or it will be found on the wrong side of history. Our grandchildren will ask, "Where did you stand on the issue when all that was going on? Did you speak up for those who were discriminated against by the church?" How will we hope to answer them?

MY FUTURE

I STILL CONSIDER MYSELF a Methodist and a minister. I am a United Methodist minister. It's all I know how to be. I still consider myself ordained by the power of God. And I see my future as a United Methodist minister.

But I feel like I have a new role since the trial. Because I'm known for the stance I took at the trial and everything that happened afterward, I have become an LGBTQ spokesperson on the national church level. And I will always be that. I have every intention of continuing my activism and standing with and for our LGBT brothers and sisters. There's no going back now. And I'm happy to do it.

I truly believe that we are at a tipping point. I believe we need to do everything in our power as United Methodists to take our church back, to get rid of the homophobic language that was put into the *Book of Discipline* in 1972. We have been in homophobic captivity too long. It's time for us to stand up and say, "Enough is enough."

People sometimes ask me if I have any regrets, and for the most part I don't. I am proud of the stand I took for my son. I'm proud to be able to take a stand now for equality and inclusion. The one regret I have today is that I did not speak out sooner and more clearly.

I thought ministering in a more conservative congregation meant that I had to stifle my own beliefs. I didn't want to push an issue that had the potential to divide the church. And, frankly, I was afraid. As a family man, I was concerned about my security. Sometimes I managed to slip in subtle pleas for tolerance into my sermons. But mostly I was silent.

I do regret not saying out loud in the congregation something like, "I know there may be some of us here who are struggling with the issue of sexuality identity. That's okay. No matter where you come out, this is not your choice. This is the way God created you. And God doesn't create junk. *You are created in the image of God*, no matter whether you're homosexual or heterosexual or bisexual or transgender. You are a beloved child of God."

I wish I had said something like that. I don't know how many people, especially young people, were struggling in my congregation. And maybe they were just waiting for a word from their pastor.

I will never be silent again. I will not simply stand by and be a silent supporter. My trial has shown me that I am stronger than I knew I was. And the need for people to speak out is here right now.

I think The United Methodist Church has incredible potential. I *chose* this church as my faith tradition because of that potential. For the most part, United Methodists are people of great faith. Their religion is a religion of the heart. It's genuine. It comes from the right place.

I am so encouraged by the reconciling church movement in The United Methodist Church. There are 500-plus reconciling United Methodist churches in the United States. Of course, that's out of some 30,000 United Methodist churches in the country, which doesn't seem like a lot. But since the recent publicity surrounding LGBT issues in The United Methodist Church, including my trial, that movement has really accelerated. There are so many churches now in the process of becoming reconciling churches.

Not long ago, I preached at First United Methodist Church of Germantown, Pennsylvania, on a Sunday following an RMN seminar. More than thirty people from nine different churches attended, and all of those churches are now en route to becoming reconciling churches. And that's just in Eastern Pennsylvania.

RMN has reportedly gotten so many requests from United Methodist churches to inquire about the process that they've had to hire new people to be able to facilitate. If my trial turns out to have had an influence on this development, that alone would have been worth the sacrifices.

I know there will be change. Change is coming. And my pledge to my children, my family, my LGBT brothers and sisters in the church and beyond, is that I will work hard to be a part of that change.

It's high time for the church to denounce hatred and discrimination. It's time to embrace our diversity and to heal the wounds we have inflicted on others out of ignorance and fear. It's time to stand firmly on the side of love.

The biggest lesson I have learned from my experience is that you have to follow your heart; you have to stand up for what you believe is right. It's not always easy to do that. In fact, it's never easy to take a stand against discrimination. Society is always putting pressure on us to maintain the status quo. In my case, sadly, it was The United Methodist Church that exerted such pressure on me. If you take a stand for love and justice, you're risking a lot, sometimes even your life. Institutions will threaten to take your paycheck, your career, your security. The government may threaten to penalize you or imprison you. Even individuals may threaten you.

But if you want to be a part of transforming this world, if you want to live without regrets over missed opportunities, you must follow your heart; you must take a stand. I dare say that if you live in the United States, your courageous stance will be seen and it will be supported. You may lose your job, you may lose some friends, even family, but you will be rewarded and supported.

Be courageous, take the risk that God put before you, follow your heart, and take a stand for love and justice. God will not let you down!

EPILOGUE

> Darkness cannot drive out darkness, only light can do that. Hatred cannot drive out hatred, only love can do that.
>
> — Dr. Martin Luther King, Jr.

AN INTRIGUING THING happened immediately after my trial was over: Jon Boger, the man who had filed the complaint against me, came over to where I was seated in the courtroom and said, "I hope you know this is nothing personal."

I said, "Absolutely, you don't even know me. I don't know you. How can it be personal?"

And then we shook hands.

Many people have asked me how I was able to smile at him and shake his hand after all that he had done to me.

Looking back on it now, I do have to say that the confrontations had felt personal at times. But throughout this whole ordeal I tried hard—with God's help—to take the high road. I was able to take the attacks on my character, on my family, and on my ministry and process them in a positive way. I did feel terrorized and unsafe at times. I felt anger and frustration. But I never allowed myself to dwell on the negative, and I was always able to respond with love.

What did I do? I journaled, I communicated my anger and frustrations with friends, and I hit the crap out of that poor little yellow ball during my tennis matches. Mentally, I tried to stay focused on the bigger picture. I told myself that all this would be over, one way or another, in a matter of months. No matter what the outcome of the trial, the struggle would be over. I tried to create positive spaces and do "happy things," such as going for walks, listening to music, playing my guitars, and watching funny movies.

All of this helped me to stay positive. When you allow negative feelings to take root in yourself, you cannot even see the doors that may be right in front of you. If you dwell on the negative, you're too occupied wondering why the door behind you closed, and you may be trying to get back through the closed door in vain. Most of the time we can choose our paths forward, for, as we move on, we will find new doors that may open up new and exciting possibilities for our lives.

For me such possibilities opened up as I grew into a new role and a new understanding of my calling and ministry. I was becoming an advocate and activist for LGBT rights. Through press interviews and networking with LGBT groups and organizations, I became widely known as "the minister who was being put on trial." I gained a new perspective, a bird's eye perspective. First, I received so much support and encouragement from like-minded folks within the larger church network and beyond, and, second, I was beginning to become a part of human rights planning and action sessions.

I started to focus on the positive, as I was able to discover and walk through new doors, which led me to take the high road of love and forgiveness toward those who were attacking my character. And that was something people noticed. I got comments such as, "Where do you get the strength to continue in your ministry with all that you're being put through?" And, "How come you can stay so positive, even loving, when you are under attack like that?"

People watch us, especially when we're facing hardships and animosity; they're watching us to see how we deal with those difficult challenges in life, because we all face them at one time or another. Unbeknownst to me at first, people were watching me and, as I was able to take the high road and respond with love and positive strength to serious animosities, they took inspiration from my attitude.

And that, in turn, led to a whole new and exciting ministry for me that takes me around the country to speak and bring healing to many who have been and continue to be hurt by religious institutions. And I am privileged to be a part of changing the world and the church toward a better future, a time when nobody will be rejected, refused, or ridiculed because of their sexual orientation.

So choose love to overcome evil, fear, and hatred in the world. It's not just beneficial to your own life; your choice will also multiply the divine light that will ultimately drive out all darkness.

Amen!

RESPONSE

"Because the Northeastern Jurisdiction Committee on Appeals is scheduled to hear the appeal of Mr. Frank Schaefer as this book is going to press, it is inappropriate for me to comment. However, I can call upon all people of faith and conscience to keep Frank, his family and our United Methodist Church in earnest, loving prayer, as we try to struggle gracefully through this painful time of divisive disagreement. I pray confidently that the church may emerge stronger, more hopeful and more faithful to both its biblical grounding and its prophetic calling, as it continues to make disciples of Jesus Christ and equip them for God's transforming work in the world."

Bishop Peggy Johnson
Eastern Pennsylvania Annual Conference of
the United Methodist Church
June, 2014

APPENDIX

Excerpt from the Official Court Transcript

UNITED METHODIST CHURCH

EASTERN PENNSYLVANIA ANNUAL CONFERENCE

RE: The matter of Reverend Frank Schaefer

Rev. Schaefer's testimony to the trial court on November 19th:

BISHOP GWINN: The court will be back in session now. I'm going to recognize Reverend Coombe. Certainly he can proceed with the next witness.

REV. COOMBE: I call Reverend Frank Schaefer to be our next witness.

DIRECT EXAMINATION BY REV. COOMBE:

Q. Okay, Frank?

A. I'm good.

Q. You're here because you want to be on the stand right now for yourself, right?

A. Absolutely.

Q. Your ministry has been discussed at great length. Is there anything that you would like to say?

A. Yes. I would like to just make some general statements about my ministry as it was brought up, if I may. I am far from perfect. Let me start by saying that. I'm a human being like everybody else. And I sort of cringed in my seat when Drew said something about being the embodiment of Christ. I am a person with many faults and mistakes and I'm the first one to admit that. I need the grace of God just like everybody else. But I do think that I have a personality, and I have been given that,…that is very gregarious. It is very outreaching and extroverted. I am a person who is very nonjudgmental. I have an easy time to extend grace to anybody, even people that wrong me. I am very quick to forgive. And I think those are things that are gifts that have been given me as part of my ministry. And I think these gifts in particular have really helped me in my ministry to extend a warm welcome to everybody. I do not judge people, because I don't think that's my responsibility. I suspend judgment. I will talk with anybody. I am there to do pastoral care for everybody.

Now—and this is a true statement—I have never refused pastoral care to anybody who called me or let me know that they needed me. I was there for them. And I would do that for even people that consider me an enemy in a heartbeat. Now, where I draw the line—and maybe that's where a misunderstanding may have come in in earlier testimony—where I draw the line is I am not a trained counselor. Sometimes I will say to people, look, I am doing pastoral care and I'm here to listen to you and speak with you and pray with you and encourage you. But I am not a trained counselor. And so sometimes I refer people to professionals, either Christian professionals or some other professionals, that have a therapy background and training. I really do feel called—I am not just saying that—to minister to all people, to everybody regardless of gender, race, nationality, economic status, and sexual orientation. I do feel that call is not just something I am saying. It is something I am living and breathing and it's something I totally believe in. That defines my ministry.

When I was ministering at the Iona church—and now I have done that for eleven years—I have truly embraced everybody. It doesn't matter to me where people come from politically or in their theology. I minister to everybody. And so I found it interesting that after a few years, this actually led to a very interesting texture of people that we attracted to the church. Everybody seemed to be attracted to our ministry. And people became very open through my teaching on openness and inclusiveness as well as my personal outreach to people that came in as visitors. We all of a sudden had people of color coming to our service, which is quite rare in Pennsylvania Dutch country. We had people of different sexual orientations coming in.

And what happened at the same time was that the congregation was changing and was becoming more accepting. And I will never forget one Sunday not too far in the distance—it may have been last year in November in a communion service—when one lesbian sister that had joined in membership with her partner and was now a member of our congregation had, prior to the service, suffered a stroke and was discharged just a couple of days before this communion Sunday. She had some trouble with walking. She literally had to say out loud the word "step" so that her brain would process the command and actually her leg would take a step forward. It was so important for this sister to be part of the sacrament of communion. She stepped—literally stepped all the way up the aisle toward the altar saying "step, step, step" every step of the way.

When people around her saw that—and I am talking about some people that were opposed to homosexuals to being a part of the church, being members of the church, or having rights—I noticed that as she approached the altar area, there was sobbing in the room. And I noticed that people were grabbing handkerchiefs and napkins and wiping the tears off their faces. This act of coming toward the altar of this young lesbian sister but wanting communion so badly that she was there even in her illness changed the minds and hearts of many that morning.

And that is the kind of congregation that we became at IUM. I'm not here to say everything was a-okay in our congregation. There's always been struggle too. And I think that's unfortunately a reality of every church. But I have really tried to listen to everybody and to get everybody's input. And I think some of the people that testified this morning, they know that too. I can mention some examples, but I am not going to because that is not really what this is about.

I'm here to tell you that what makes up my ministry is a ministry of inclusiveness. I love every single person. And that's what my ministry really is about: unconditional love.

Now, I have to tell you—and I know you wanted to ask me the question. I am just going to skip that. I have to tell you what happened to me since the complaint was filed against me. We had a congregational meeting on May 2nd. And at that meeting it was announced what I did. As you have heard, initially there was a lot of support. But what happened was that as I indicated in my written statement to the Bishop at the cabinet, I was certainly not going to lie about what I did if somebody asked me about it. And I was certainly not going to lie about my position, my theological position. Once this became known, people did ask me. People in my church asked me. Eventually the press asked me. And I found myself being transformed into something that was totally new to me. I became an advocate for gays, lesbians, transgenders, and bisexual people. I became a spokesperson for them. And I embraced that because I saw that as a new calling from God. I received I don't know how many dozens of letters and cards, e-mails, Facebook messages of people that are hurting. LGBT people, their parents, their relatives. And many of them shared stories with me that were so sad. Stories of rejection, of discrimination, of being harmed. And I am a minister. I was called to be a minister by God first and by The United Methodist Church after that. I have to minister to those who hurt. And that's what I'm doing. That's my new understanding of my calling that God has given me. I have to minister to my brothers and sisters that hurt. And just as transparent as it was back in 2006 to my superiors, I have to be transparent to you, too, the jury, because you have to make a decision today. And I will let you know that I cannot go back to be a silent supporter. I am now an advocate. This is a new role into which I am finding myself and I am accepting this as a calling from God. I must continue to speak for my brothers and sisters who are LGBT in this world and especially in The United Methodist Church.

So before you make a decision, please know that I will continue to minister to all people equally regardless of their gender, nationality, race, social status, economic status, or sexual orientation. And my message is going to be that we as a church and as individuals need to stop judging people based on their sexual orientation or anything else. We have to stop the hate speech. We have to stop treating them as second-class Christians. We have to stop harming beloved children of God. We have to reach out to them and treat them as Jesus would have treated them. That's going to be my message.

I don't think things happen by chance. I was given a stole and it is a rainbow stole. And if I am permitted, Bishop, to wear it, I would like to put this on me as a sign that I will make a covenant from this day forth never to be silent again. Is it okay, Bishop, to put that on me?

BISHOP GWINN: I have ruled that the rainbow color is not an offense to what we're doing here and it is permissible to have a rainbow color on.

REV. SCHAEFER: I would wear this as a visible symbol for you to understand that this is what I have to do from now on. That's all I have to say.

REV. COOMBE: Thank you. I have no more questions.

BISHOP GWINN: All right. Thank you, Reverend Coombe. And Reverend Fisher?

CROSS-EXAMINATION BY REV. FISHER:

Q. Well, in light of your statement just now, maybe this is going to be easy. I thought maybe we would need to bring in some media quotes.

REV. FISHER: By the way, my apologies to the media. I read the newspaper all the time and I believe most of what I see there. My apologies to the media. That was a throwaway line. Don't take it too seriously.

BY REV. FISHER:

Q. I guess I need to ask you, Frank, in light of your declared position, you realize that you put yourself at odds with the *Book of Discipline* of The United Methodist Church as it currently stands with the General Conference declaring certain boundaries for ministerial behavior?

A. I would have to disagree with that statement.

Q. Let me ask you some concrete versions of that. You've been tried and found guilty of violating two provisions of the *Book of Discipline*. So I would ask you: Are you willing to repent of your actions you have been found guilty of and renounce your disobedience to the discipline of The United Methodist Church?

A. I cannot.

Q. Will you promise from henceforth never to perform another same-sex wedding and ceremony and from henceforth to uphold all the provisions of the discipline?

A. I cannot make that statement.

REV. FISHER: Thank you. That's all the church has to ask.

BISHOP GWINN: All right. Redirect please?

REV. COOMBE: I have no further questions.

BISHOP GWINN: I am conferring with my counsel. The jury had asked a question that's fairly close to what the counsel for the church just asked. And I'm of the opinion it's been answered, your question has been answered. Yes, Reverend Coombe?

REV. COOMBE: I have no further questions, if you want to dismiss.

BISHOP GWINN: All right. And both counsels are ready to dismiss the witness?

REV. FISHER: Yes.

BISHOP GWINN: You may be excused, Reverend Schaefer. Thank you.